THE BEACHES

Creation of a Toronto Neighbourhood

The Beaches

Creation of a Toronto Neighbourhood

RICHARD WHITE

UNIVERSITY OF TORONTO PRESS
Toronto Buffalo London

Toronto Buffalo London
utorontopress.com
Printed in Canada

ISBN 978-1-4875-0894-4 (cloth)
ISBN 978-1-4875-2646-7 (paper)
ISBN 978-1-4875-3937-5 (EPUB)
ISBN 978-1-4875-3936-8 (PDF)

Library and Archives Canada Cataloguing in Publication
Title: The Beaches : creation of a Toronto neighbourhood / Richard White.
Names: White, Richard, 1952– author.
Description: Includes bibliographical references and index.
Identifiers: Canadiana (print) 20240305078 | Canadiana (ebook) 20240305418 | ISBN 9781487508944 (hardcover) | ISBN 9781487526467 (softcover) | ISBN 9781487539375 (EPUB) | ISBN 9781487539368 (PDF)
Subjects: LCSH: Beaches (Toronto, Ont.) – History. | LCSH: Toronto (Ont.) – History.
Classification: LCC FC3097.52 .W45 2024 | DDC 971.3/541 – dc23

Cover design: Val Cooke
Cover images: William Kurelek, *The Boardwalk at Toronto's Beaches*, 1974, mixed media, 53.8 × 43.8 cm, © The Estate of William Kurelek, courtesy of the Wynick/Tuck Gallery, Toronto; Val Cooke

We wish to acknowledge the land on which the University of Toronto Press operates. This land is the traditional territory of the Wendat, the Anishnaabeg, the Haudenosaunee, the Métis, and the Mississaugas of the Credit First Nation.

This book has been published with the help of a grant from the Federation for the Humanities and Social Sciences, through the Awards to Scholarly Publications Program, using funds provided by the Social Sciences and Humanities Research Council of Canada.

University of Toronto Press acknowledges the financial support of the Government of Canada, the Canada Council for the Arts, and the Ontario Arts Council, an agency of the Government of Ontario, for its publishing activities.

Canada Council for the Arts | Conseil des Arts du Canada

ONTARIO ARTS COUNCIL
CONSEIL DES ARTS DE L'ONTARIO
an Ontario government agency
un organisme du gouvernement de l'Ontario

Funded by the Government of Canada | Financé par le gouvernement du Canada | Canada

FSC www.fsc.org MIX Paper | Supporting responsible forestry FSC® C016245

Contents

Acknowledgments

Although this book is a work of history written by a historian, it owes a great deal to the geographer Ted Relph, a pioneer of urban landscape studies, especially his informal but truly exceptional *Toronto Guide*, written over thirty years ago. Ted was kind enough to read and comment on an early draft of this book, as was another accomplished urban geographer, Richard Harris, whose advice, especially on the book's appendix, was nothing less than essential. I am grateful to both scholars for their guidance. The publisher's two anonymous readers also made valuable comments on the original draft, prompting me to dig deeper into the neighbourhood's social makeup and evolution. The public-facing staff at the City of Toronto Archives and the special collections staff at the Toronto Reference Library have been very helpful in preparing the image files, and Haydn Lawrence, my colleague at University of Toronto Scarborough, kindly and expertly prepared the book's maps. I would also like to acknowledge the important work done over the years by the devoted neighbourhood historians Barbara Myrvold and Mary Campbell, whose publications both inspired and informed me in the early stages of my research.

THE BEACHES

Creation of a Toronto Neighbourhood

Introduction

The Beaches is one of Toronto's best known and most admired neighbourhoods. Even people who have never set foot in it often nod in approval when they hear its name. Why should this be? The neighbourhood has no striking works of architecture or elegant public spaces, no must-see galleries or public institutions, and no associations with historic events or famous people – except for maybe Glenn Gould – all the sorts of things that create neighbourhood reputations and draw visitors to them.

It does, of course, have a beach (or beaches, see note below), something of a novelty for a large metropolis in the middle of a continent and this, on its own, might give the neighbourhood some profile. To those who have spent time alongside the ocean, the neighbourhood's beach can be a disappointment, for like most freshwater, tideless beaches it has scant marine ambience and can seem rather lifeless. Moreover, the lake it borders is usually so cold that anyone opting for a dip will likely be in and out rather quickly, on even the hottest summer days, making it a hard place to luxuriate in "beach" culture. Yet there can be no doubt that as a place to soak up sun, watch clouds, feel fresh breezes, and generally enjoy a lakeside environment – if not to swim – the neighbourhood's beach and beachside boardwalk have long been, and still are, part of its reputation and appeal.

But the beach is not the Beaches. The Beaches, as the name is used today, is a residential neighbourhood; it borders the lake but extends about a kilometre inland from it, meaning much of the neighbourhood is actually some distance from the beach. People can go to the Beaches without going to the beach. The question then becomes what makes this larger built-up area so attractive, and the answer, most people would agree, is its *character* – a hard to define quality that results not from the lake or the beach per se, though they contribute, but from a blend of all its natural and man-made elements. While this character might not be enough to draw international tourists – indeed the Beaches has not a single hotel so it cannot draw tourists in the way distinctive neighbourhoods in major cities do – it has been enough to make the neighbourhood attractive to generations of Torontonians as a place to live and visit. This character – one might call it charm – is the essence of the Beaches and probably the main source of its present-day popularity.

To a historian of urban form, this raises an obvious set of questions – how, when, and why did this character emerge?

And perhaps more fundamentally, can history help identify what, precisely, this character is?

***

The Beaches occupies land along the north shore of Lake Ontario some seven or eight kilometres east of Toronto's core; it is roughly rectangular in shape, about two kilometres east to west and, as noted, extends about one kilometre north from the lake. The first third of that one kilometre, closest to the lake, is a low, mostly level plain, rising gradually but never gaining an elevation much above the beach, especially in its western half, while the remaining two-thirds consists of a hill rising some thirty metres, in some places quite steeply, and a resulting upper plain. The land drains directly into the lake, meaning it is, or at least was, traversed by several south-flowing streams which, in descending the hill and passing through the lower plain, created a terrain more varied than a simplified description suggests. The neighbourhood is, and always has been, purely residential; it has never had any industry, and its commerce has always been small-scale and confined to the main east-west thoroughfare, Queen Street. Its population currently stands at about 21,000, significantly less than at its peak, in the 1940s, of 26,000.[1] But this decline has resulted from decreasing family and household (which includes renters and boarders) size, not from the abandonment or loss of housing. Almost every square metre of the Beaches today is healthy urban fabric.

The area began to emerge as an identifiable district early in the nineteenth century, shortly after the British established the colony of Upper Canada, designated the Town of York as its seat of government, and began granting land around the town to private owners. We know little about who initially occupied or cultivated what is now the Beaches, but signs are that through the first half of the nineteenth century it remained a sparsely settled, underdeveloped, semi-rural district, owned not by enterprising pioneer farmers but by well-connected speculators waiting for land values to rise. In the final third of the century, it began serving as a seasonal recreation area for city residents, initially with commercial amusement grounds and then, in the 1890s, private lakefront cottages. By 1900, with the city expanding rapidly in all directions and street railway service not far behind, the district's landowners began subdividing and selling their property for residential development, such that by 1914 the Beaches had become a residential neighbourhood in the east end of Toronto with a permanent population in the thousands. It was further built up and populated in the generation that followed, and by 1940, with houses covering the land on both the upper and lower plains, and on the hill itself, the neighbourhood we know today had come to be.

The Beaches is often described as having the look and feel of the lakeside cottage community it once was, an enduring bit of local lore that has some, but not much, basis in fact. Admittedly, some vestiges of its summer recreation era do survive. And the neighbourhood does look and feel like an aging Ontario town, with its highly conventional housing and outmoded main street, along with its low proportion of recent immigrants and visible minorities – among the lowest in all of Toronto.[2] But the truth is that next to nothing of what one sees in the neighbourhood today dates from its summer cottage years.

What one does see today is the "streetcar suburb" that supplanted the short-lived recreational communities. This label, bestowed by urban historians on late-nineteenth-century residential areas built at the edge of cities in response to streetcar extensions, fits the Beaches hand in glove. The rectilinear street grid, the narrow building lots, the nearly endless rows of houses extending lot line to lot line with no orientation to the lake – these are not the work of individuals building summer cottages but of entrepreneurial landowners, subdividers, and builders responding to Edwardian Toronto's booming housing market. Some of the old wooden-clad houses resemble summer cottages, but nearly all of them were built as year-round houses by, or to sell to, the emerging urban middle class. Walking about the neighbourhood today, observing all this, one would never think one was in a cottage community. The lake and beach are never far away, of course, in fact or in mind, but the neighbourhood is, and has been since it was built, a residential suburb.

***

A neighbourhood history is premised on the notion that there is such a thing as a "neighbourhood," and before moving to the body of this work it is worth exploring briefly what the word means and how it will be employed.[3] A dictionary definition begins "a number of people forming a loosely cohesive community within a larger unit" and then goes on for another eighty words, adding but then qualifying other features.[4] Evidently the word is not easily defined. Faced with such equivocation, one is tempted to fall back on a common-sense definition – a part of a city with a name, bordered usually by a major road or rail line or a natural feature such as a body of water or a steep hill. But if a neighbourhood is to be a substantive thing it must be more than just an area; it needs some sort of defining quality or feature. Functioning as a social unit, as the dictionary definition suggests, might be that defining feature – a community within which residents socialize, attend school, and purchase goods and services. Modern urban planners, taking cues from an earlier, less mobile time, have been envisioning such neighbourhoods for decades but have seldom managed to coax them into existence.[5] Perhaps there was a time when neighbourhoods functioned this way, but they no longer do. Present-day city dwellers, especially the middle class, invariably socialize, shop, obtain professional and artisanal services, seek out schools, and engage with institutions throughout the city; indeed, many now consider shopping or schooling their children locally to be rather parochial.[6] Neither social nor functional coherence defines a modern neighbourhood.

A more realistic definition is an urban area with an observable physical or social quality – an area of expensive homes on large lots, an area laid out and built at a particular time, an area in which people of a certain class or ethnicity predominate.[7] This definition has problems too: boundaries of such neighbourhoods are difficult to determine, and big-city neighbourhoods are almost never socially or stylistically homogeneous. But its imprecision, together with its dependence on visual observation rather than serious analysis, makes it easy to employ. For better or worse, *character* of this sort is the basis for many of the world's best-known neighbourhoods, and Toronto's are no exception. Names such as Rosedale, Cabbagetown, Little Italy – and the Beaches – refer to neighbourhoods with a certain look or feel and a degree of class commonality, but for which nobody, neither locals nor social scientists, would or could assign precise boundaries or observe significant functional cohesion.[8]

A casual definition is fine for everyday speech, and this history was initially conceived with such a definition in mind. But as work progressed it became evident that precise, consistently applied boundaries were needed for some of the research, such as analysing plans of subdivision, assessing the impact of municipal services, and counting and categorizing residents' employment. Accordingly, precise boundaries were drawn, arbitrary though they may be. The Beaches in this history is the curve-topped rectangle bounded by present-day Woodbine Avenue (on the west), Kingston Road (north), Victoria Park Avenue (east) and Lake Ontario (south). This excludes two areas sometimes considered part of the Beaches: a triangle of land to the west customarily known as the beach triangle and a substantial square of land to the east often called Fallingbrook. Some books on the Beaches include either or both of those areas; this one does not.

***

This book has been crafted as a work of analytical narrative history – it tells something of a story, in loosely chronological sequence, but with frequent diversions to explore themes, make arguments, and offer conclusions. It is based on a range of official documents such as council minutes, assessment rolls, city directories, early plans of subdivision, and the census, but also, occasionally, on historical newspapers – tantalizingly accessible and searchable now through digitization – and, more frequently, on a close examination of historical photographs and the landscape itself. Its overall objective is

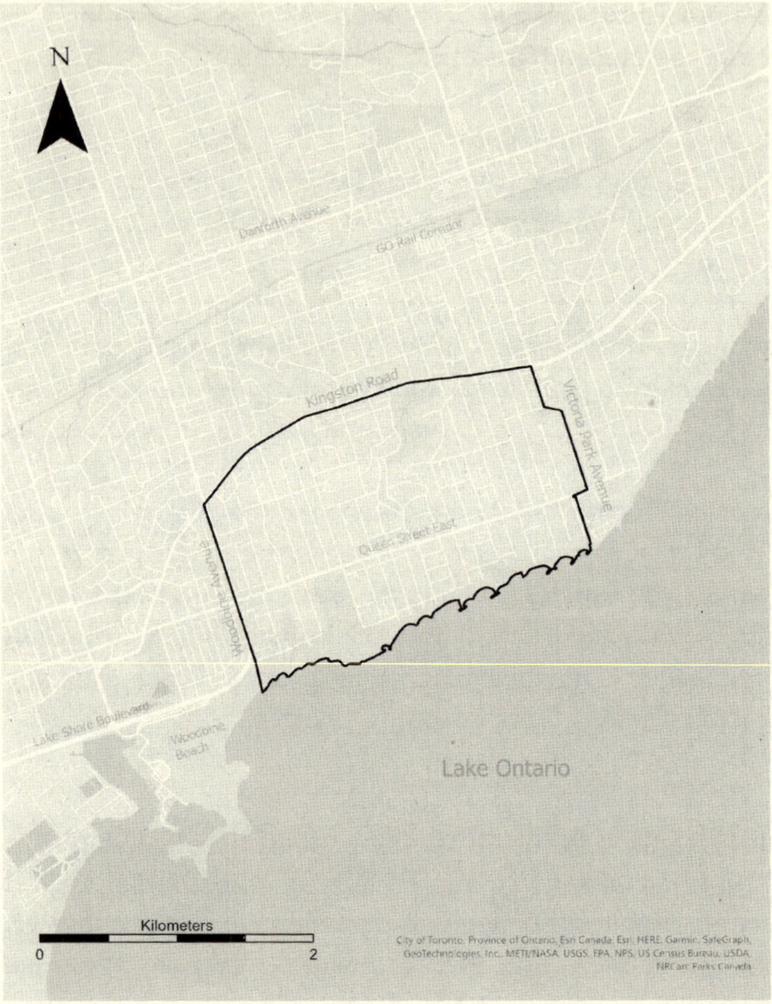

Map 1. The Beaches Neighbourhood: Downtown Toronto (Queen and Yonge Streets) is 7.5 kilometres west of the neighbourhood centre.

to recount how, when, and why the neighbourhood came to acquire its character, by which is meant primarily physical character but also, to a degree, socio-demographic character for as the accomplished historian of urban form Spiro Kostoff once reminded us, "Cities are amalgams of buildings and people."[9] Since that character was set by about 1940, or so this analysis concludes, the detailed narrative draws to a close then. It goes on to make observations about the neighbourhood after the Second World War – exploring what has changed and what has not – but with nothing like the detail presented about its formative years.

One aspect of the neighbourhood that this book leaves unexplored is how it compares with other Toronto neighbourhoods built at about the same time. Is the Beaches unique, or is it typical? How much of what is recounted here occurred in other city neighbourhoods? No doubt there are similarities and differences between the Beaches and other neighbourhoods, both in the forces that shaped them and in the product that resulted, and elucidating these would be a valuable undertaking. Indeed, friends and colleagues who discussed or read early drafts of this book have often commented on the value of such a comparison. But no attempt has been made to do so. Meaningful comparisons would require a mountain of additional research, and in the end such a pursuit would turn this book into something it was not meant to be. Two recent published neighbourhood histories cover ground comparable to what is examined here: Carolyn Whitzman's academic monograph on Parkdale and Joanne Doucette's self-published but impressively researched book on Leslieville.[10] Both provided food for thought, but the task of comparing these or any other neighbourhoods to the Beaches is left to others.

The final chapter offers something rather unusual for a narrative history: it examines the present-day neighbourhood through a cultural landscape lens. The concept of cultural landscapes, developed and refined within the disciplines of human geography and landscape architecture over the last fifty years, extends the word "landscape" beyond its traditional association with nature to include places created or significantly altered by human agency. Cultural landscapes, in the words of the UNESCO body that formally designates such places, are "combined works of nature and humankind," and one of this body's sub-definitions takes the centrality of human agency even further, including landscapes that have been "designed and created intentionally by man."[11] This is how the concept and term are employed here, encompassing fully urban places such as residential streetscapes, public parks, and commercial storefronts. This broadening of the word "landscape" makes good sense when one considers how much of the world – even seemingly natural places like the rural countryside or a mountain park – has been touched by human hands. Cultural landscapes, or what in cities are often called urban landscapes, are what most of us see, day in and day out, whenever we open our eyes outdoors.

One of the key forces behind the emergence of cultural landscape studies is historical preservationism. A wish to preserve, or somehow steward, cultural landscapes is often what prompts the study of them, something that is hard to overlook in the mission statements of institutions such as the UNESCO body cited above or the US-based Cultural Landscape Foundation.[12] But this history of the Beaches has no connection whatsoever to the preservationist mindset. It makes no attempt to portray the landscapes described herein as worthy of preservation. It simply recounts and analyses their creation. In fact, if anything, by uncovering the complexity of the neighbourhood's history, this study shows how misleading the preservation of individual bits of it can be.

Another of the field's foundational principles is that man-made landscapes, like any historical artifact, reveal something about the collective culture that created them, and this founding principle is fully espoused here. The final chapter, which employs the urban landscapes lens, uses the present-day landscape mainly to recapitulate key themes in the historical narrative but also to identify some aspects of the people who created the neighbourhood. This is all possible, and fruitful, because the neighbourhood has changed so little since its creation; indeed, its founding principles are on clear display in the present-day landscapes – a revealing detail not about the people who created the landscapes but about the people who subsequently inhabited it.

A Note on the Name

One cannot write about Toronto's Beaches neighbourhood without commenting, and taking a position, on its name – the singular Beach or plural Beaches, a matter of serious dispute among many residents, and a cause of serious eye-rolling among most non-residents. This study stands firmly on the side of the latter name, as its title shows, and does so for mostly historical reasons. For years there was no name at all for the undeveloped and scarcely inhabited lakefront lands east of the city. As it developed into a recreational area in the later years of the nineteenth century it had two main foci, a beach in the east end called Balmy Beach and one at the western end called Kew Beach. There were, in other words, two beaches. But most people who came out to swim or picnic, or even to sojourn for an entire season, went to just one, either Kew or Balmy, not both – to the singular Beach, in other words, not the Beaches. As the area evolved into a larger, more settled community in the early twentieth century, however, it was generally called the Beaches, because the community encompassed more than one beach. Newspaper columns reported social life in the Beaches, the City of Toronto built a Beaches public library in 1909, and the Harbour Commissioners planned improvements to the eastern beaches in 1912. Other official documents and debates employed this term. The singular name remained in local use, however, perhaps because of a lingering attachment, among some older residents at least, to one of the beaches. Then in the 1940s and 1950s it seems to have become common as a name for the overall neighbourhood. Why this occurred, and on what grounds it was defended – it is somewhat ahistorical – has not emerged in researching this book, but this singular name was common enough in the formative years of the current generation of aging, historically minded residents that they demanded it be made official, and they have partially succeeded. Though I too am an aging, historically minded resident, I have not been persuaded. For this history, which covers the genesis and growth of one neighbourhood out of multiple beaches, Beaches seemed right, on account of both basic logic and historical usage.

Map 2. Reference Maps

Present-day neighbourhood, western section

Present-day neighbourhood, central section

Present-day neighbourhood, eastern section

CHAPTER ONE

Claiming and Founding

The founding and early development of Upper Canada has been closely examined by generations of Canadian historians, Upper Canada being the seed from which English Canada grew and thus the place to look for some sort of national DNA. And since the Town of York (Toronto as of 1834) was the political and commercial heart of Upper Canada, and the Beaches is now one its better-known neighbourhoods, one might expect the early history of the Beaches to have been correspondingly well explored. But that is not the case. Although the land that would become the Beaches was nearly all granted to private owners by 1800, we know next to nothing of its history prior to the mid-nineteenth century. Research for this study has uncovered the names of some of the early landowners, and more could be found in archival records – should any historian take the time to do so – but who actually lived on the land in that half-century or more, and how they used it, will likely remain unknown for all time.

For centuries before any colonial land grants were issued, Indigenous North American people had been living on and using the land along the north shore of Lake Ontario; these were primarily Iroquoian-speakers prior to and at the time of first European contact, and Algonquian-speaking Mississauga, migrants from the north, when settlement began in the eighteenth century.[1] Awareness of this fact has increased as historians have become more open to including Indigenous North Americans in Canada's historical narrative and archaeologists have identified and interpreted more archaeological sites. Knowledge remains limited, however, and confined to certain locations. To date no significant material evidence has been unearthed of Indigenous activity on the land defined in this study as the Beaches. Yet considering the substantial pre-contact population that archaeologists hypothesize for the region – perhaps 25,000 on lands north of Lake Ontario[2] – there can be no doubt that the roughly two kilometres of shoreland, from the sandspit enclosing Ashbridge's marsh in the west to the towering Scarborough bluffs in the east, has long been travelled through, gathered from, hunted on, fished along, and probably at times settled upon by Indigenous inhabitants. Evidence of this undoubtedly exists beneath the houses and streets.

Also increasingly recognized – though in truth long observed by conscientious historians – is that much of Canada's early history is intertwined with those original inhabitants; the fur trade, for instance, clearly was founded on Indigenous knowledge and labour, and early pioneers often adopted Indigenous techniques for living with and protecting themselves from the natural environment.[3] What is perhaps new is that this perspective is beginning to alter our understanding of Canadian city-building.[4] In some cases, descendants of Indigenous inhabitants claim their people were inadequately compensated for land on which cities were built, leading to questions about the current tenure of urban land. Transportation routes and public spaces in some modern cities are now understood to be based on pre-contact Indigenous land uses or post-contact Indigenous/European interactions. Some of the names that colonial authorities applied to urban places and natural features derive from Indigenous words – not least the name Toronto.[5] All of this is now "written into" Toronto's history.[6]

But one cannot avoid the fact that Canada's commercial-industrial cities were made by and for the trans-Atlantic migrants who began arriving in and staking claims to these lands late in the eighteenth century and who, over time, produced what is now referred to as a settler society. We see no signs of the displaced Mississauga taking part in the planning or building of Toronto, or of the landowners, commercial builders, tradesmen, and day labourers who built the city adopting the techniques of or considering the wishes and needs of those previous inhabitants. And once built, the population of late Victorian and Edwardian Toronto included a minuscule number of Indigenous residents.[7] The history of an urban neighbourhood such as the Beaches is thus, in short, a chronicle of the thoughts and actions of the interlopers who comprised the settler society, and its history thus begins with their arrival. As questionable, even unjust, as the entire colonial endeavour now appears to many historians, these thoughts and actions have shaped, in this case, the living conditions and lives of tens of thousands of residents for over a hundred years, right through to the present day, and as such they warrant being recounted and analysed in some detail.

***

France was the first European power to lay claim to the north shore of Lake Ontario, for this stretch of land was a small part of the vast inland trading network established by Montreal-based French merchants in the seventeenth and eighteenth centuries. France's claim had next to no settlement associated with it, as it was essentially a commercial rather than a territorial claim, but it was internationally recognized nonetheless. In 1763, however, France was compelled to cede nearly all its North American territory to the British under the terms that ended the Seven Years' War, and the British then began the complex task of incorporating it into their own empire. Britain's main concern in the St. Lawrence/Great Lakes part of its newly acquired territory was what to do with the well-established, French-speaking, mostly rural, settlement downstream from Montreal – what was then and is still known as New France. The unsettled north shore of Lake Ontario, hundreds of kilometres further inland, drew little attention. At least not until 1783, when the formation of an independent United States, with Lake Ontario as its northern border, suddenly made that lake's north shore strategically critical territory. Accordingly, in 1787, the British struck a treaty with the area's principal

Indigenous occupants, the Mississauga, under which they acquired title to most of the lake's northern shore, at least so they believed.[8] A few years later, in 1791, the British constituted the new colony of Upper Canada, established the town of York as its administrative centre, and began surveying land on either side of the town in preparation for the influx of settlers they hoped would populate the territory and secure the colony.[9] Britain's colonial project, based on settlement, was going to be different from France's.

The Beaches emerged as a distinct place from the start of the British regime, due partly to its physical geography and partly to the actions of colonial administrators. Land around the Town of York, as in most of Upper Canada, was surveyed into rectangular lots of 200 acres, twenty survey chains (1,320 feet) wide and one hundred chains (6,600 feet) long. East of town the surveyors ran an east-west "baseline" slightly inshore from the lake and laid out lots north and south of this line, with every fifth north-south lot division designated as a public road allowance. The Beaches neighbourhood would develop on both sides of this baseline (later named Queen Street) between the road allowances that would become Woodbine and Victoria Park Avenues (figure 1).[10] Lots below the baseline were much smaller than those north of it and, given the irregular shoreline, were of varying size. All these lots would have been granted to private owners soon after being surveyed. A full slate of grantees and subsequent purchasers of Beaches lots has never been compiled, but most whose names have come to light were members of the colony's early political, military, and business elite.[11] Upper Canada's initial land grants are

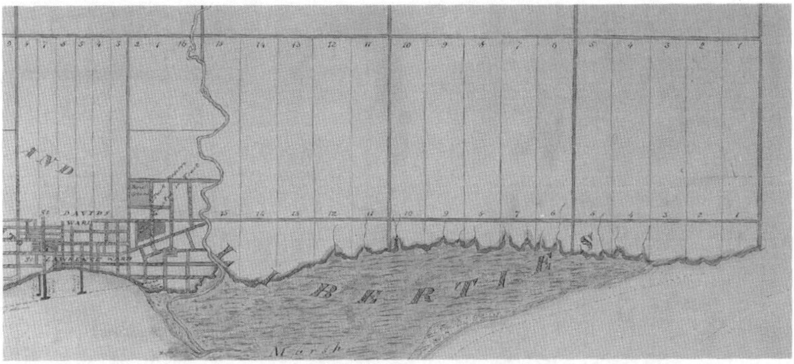

Figure 1. Detail from J.G. Chewett, "City of Toronto and Its Liberties," 1834. Central and eastern portion of the City of Toronto upon its incorporation, 1834, showing the surveyed lots of York Township, east of the city. The Beaches neighbourhood would develop in Lots 1 through 5, between the two easternmost north-south road allowances on this map (depicted by double lines), north and south of the surveyor's baseline.

Courtesy of Toronto Public Library (Maps-R-137)

known to have been done to create and sustain a colonial elite, and what we know of initial ownership in the Beaches district certainly demonstrates this.

Colonial officials soon turned their attention to building roads to connect the fledgling Town of York with its hinterland and other towns in the new colony, and in 1799 they engaged the American settlement agent and contractor Asa Danforth to construct a road eastward, towards Kingston, along a route to be "surveyed and marked at the expense of the Government."[12] The government's surveyors, observing the substantial elevation the road had to attain by the time it reached Scarborough Township, and knowing that horse-drawn wagons could not manage steep grades, opted to start the road's ascent by veering inland onto a slightly elevated plain only a few kilometres east of town. Turning away from the lake at this point also avoided areas of wetland further east. But doing so left lakefront land beyond the turn unserved by the road. It also meant that the common features of pioneer life – the tollbooth, the traveller's inn/tavern, the mill, the village church – would appear not along the lake but inland along the Kingston Road, as it was called, and a small pioneer community, named Norway, developed on the road a little beyond the turnoff in the 1820s.

This bypassed triangle of land between the Kingston Road and the lake would become the Beaches. But as it turned out, although bypassed by the road, much of this land would be placed within the City of Toronto upon its formal incorporation in 1834, while the village of Norway would not; the Don River was made the eastern limit of most of the city, but south of the surveyor's baseline the city's "liberties" extended much further east. Why the boundary was drawn in this manner is not on record, but presumably waterfront land east of the city – most of which was actually marshfront land (figure 1) – was viewed as having some future importance.[13]

We see few signs of agriculture in the area in the decades following the issuing of land grants, and for this there are several plausible explanations. The land was locked up from the start by a well-connected elite with little inclination or need to sell, and this would have blocked working pioneers from purchasing it. Any who did gain a foothold would have been stymied by the absence of a decent road to get their produce to market; a trail of sorts ran into the district along the surveyor's baseline, but it was not the permanent road farmers needed for prompt, timely travel – indeed, it was so narrow that wagons travelling opposite directions often could not pass one another.[14] The steep hill two hundred or so metres from the lake was certainly ill-suited to cultivation, both in the physical challenges it posed for fieldwork and because its sandy soil held little organic material, while much of the level land close to the lake was too wet to farm. Surely over the course of fifty years some of the drier land was cleared and cultivated, perhaps under lease from its well-heeled landowners, but the farmers who did so have left no evidence of their efforts.

The picture becomes a little clearer after mid-century. A commercially produced map from 1860 shows existing properties and their owners, revealing that by then all the original 200-acre lots had been broken up.[15] The area south of the Kingston Road between Victoria Park and Woodbine Avenues now comprised maybe fifteen separate properties, the largest about fifty acres (figure 2). Properties running north from the baseline now extended only as far as the Kingston Road, due partly to the presence of the road itself but also likely to the Grand Trunk Railway having recently been built north of the road – the GTR's builders, facing the same terrain that road builders had faced fifty years earlier, opted for the same solution of turning their route inland upon leaving the city. Railways invariably had a large impact on land ownership and development

Figure 2. Detail from "Tremaine's Map of the County of York Canada West," 1860. Southeast corner of the county, c. 1860, showing lot lines and names of property owners. Lots are now divided by the Kingston Road. The Grand Trunk Railway (completed 1856) runs roughly parallel to, and less than a kilometre north of, the road. The village of Norway was still the only built-up part of the district.

University of Toronto Library

patterns in pioneer settlements. This decision by the GTR to veer inland rather than continue along the lake made the district the only part of Toronto with a lakeshore not used for shipping or industry. The 1860 map also reveals nearly all the landowners to be not farmers but appointed lawyers and judges, successful building contractors, and well-connected officeholders, which is to say, though the lots were smaller, the nature of land ownership had not changed in half a century.

Signs of agriculture were beginning to appear, though evidence is patchy, probably because the agriculture was too. One landowner in the east end of the district apparently had a substantial orchard, which would have been a multi-year undertaking.[16] In the 1930s one aging resident recalled fields of stumps from his childhood in the 1860s as evidence of the underdeveloped state of the district.[17] While there is no reason to doubt the veracity of his recollection one might question its implication. Commercial agriculture was clearly not as well developed here as elsewhere in the region, but an uncultivated field of stumps reveals not underdevelopment, per se, but an earlier effort at agriculture followed by abandonment and relocation, a not uncommon pioneer strategy and perhaps, in this case, a sensible response to the district's circumstances and limitations.

A military officer's reconnaissance sketch done in 1868, which by good fortune remains extant, also shows cleared land and stumps, with no indication whether crops were growing around them – he did his inspection in April – but heavy forest still standing in the eastern part of the upper plain.[18] It shows a few buildings scattered about the cleared areas, suggesting small farms, but the only significant concentration of buildings is along the Kingston Road at Norway, which had been the case for decades. Near the lakeshore his sketch depicts brushwood and marshland, alongside which is a "broom manufactory" – presumably some past pioneer's effort to turn the reeds of his wetland into a cash crop. The overall picture of the district in the late 1860s is of a largely undeveloped, barely populated pocket of land owned by a handful of well-born, or at least well-connected, men, which despite having been in private ownership for some seventy years still harboured vestiges of early pioneer life.

CHAPTER TWO

Leisure and Pleasure

Just seven kilometres west of the Beaches lay the growing city of Toronto, with its factories, offices, retail shops, banks, schools, and countless other features of modern urban life. And in the 1870s this emerging metropolis, its population by then over 50,000, began having a direct impact on the Beaches. The key force at work was the increasing number of urban residents with what we now call disposable income, for these moneyed, middle-class city-dwellers spurred into being a new sort of business venture that was the very antithesis of pioneer life – the commercial amusement park.

The first, Victoria Park, opened to the paying public in June 1878 on a lakefront site now occupied by the R.C. Harris water treatment plant, just beyond the city boundary.[1] It was established by a firm of local entrepreneurs, Boyle, Shields & Co., that leased the site from Toronto merchant

Peter Paterson, who had acquired the property several decades earlier from the Winstanley family.[2] Victoria Park's two principal structures were a grand wooden pavilion with a surrounding covered verandah which "furnished shelter for the dancers," one contemporary publication noted, and an observation tower from which one could spy the distant city.[3] Amusements ranged from a shooting gallery to donkey rides to a steam-driven merry-go-round, but the park also offered outdoor activities such as nature walks and overnight camping and, along the water, places for swimming, boating, and fishing.[4] City residents were undoubtedly the target market; the proprietors ran a scheduled passenger steamboat to their site from the city's central harbour – a half-hour trip, their advertising claimed. The park must have been a commercial success. It remained in business over twenty years.

Another quite different place of amusement appeared at about the same time – Kew Gardens, the venture of an enterprising Englishman named Joseph Williams.[5] Williams had come to Canada thirty years earlier as a young sergeant with the British army, but after marrying a local woman he chose to leave the military and remain in Canada, and in 1853 he and his wife purchased land in the Beaches district and began life as latter-day Canadian pioneers. His initial purchase was a small tract north of the baseline road (not yet Queen Street), but the following year he augmented that with a huge tract of partly swampy land south of the line that extended down to the lake.[6] He named his property Kew Farm, apparently after the gardens near London that he remembered fondly from his childhood. Like others who saw the area in the 1850s, Williams reportedly encountered plenty of bush and stumps, although the first land he bought must have had at least a partially developed farm on it because he was apparently selling produce in the city market only a year after buying it. Little is known about Williams and his farm. At some point he built a large home on his land south of Queen Street – he and his wife had a large family – and presumably he cleared more land and expanded his operations over the years. There are also signs of him and his family engaging in the popular, if risky, local pastime of land speculation, buying and selling various adjacent properties. But records of his activities are meagre.

One wonders if by the late 1870s Williams and his family had begun to feel like something of an anachronism as they watched, and no doubt heard, boatloads of tourists steaming by on their way to and from Victoria Park, about a kilometre east of their farm. In any case, whatever their thinking, soon after Victoria Park was established Williams resolved to transform his operation from market garden to pleasure garden, to sell fresh air and outdoor pleasure to the city folk, not just vegetables. And in 1879 he opened an enterprise he called Kew Gardens – applying the full London name now to a place bearing no resemblance whatsoever to its namesake – offering the public what he called "innocent amusements," perhaps an attempt to counter the unsavoury reputation that commercial amusement parks had begun to acquire.[7]

"Recreations" might have been a better word than "amusements" for although Williams did at times present live music Kew Gardens had no donkey-rides or merry-go-rounds. People came to his property to swim and to enjoy the lake breezes. But it was, like Victoria Park, a commercial venture. We do not know how or where he controlled entry, but he apparently charged admission, in 1891 at least, for a newspaper report that summer stated that "a 25-cent ticket admits to the grounds and procures a good supper, including raspberries and cream," and we know from several sources that he rented tents and cabins and sold farm-fresh meals and snacks.[8] And Williams surely had competing with Victoria Park in mind when, at the start of his second season, he advertised that passing steamboats could also dock and discharge passengers at his wharf, free of charge.[9] He seems not to have substantially altered the grounds, leaving most of the southern portion, towards the lake, as swamp and brush, but he did build wooden walkways overtop the wetlands and erect shelters and service buildings here and there.[10] His endeavour clearly caught on. Within a few years Kew Gardens was an east-end landmark and a regular spot for church picnics and athletic activities, and by the 1890s newspapers were reporting throngs of visitors on major summer holidays.[11] Kew Gardens remained in business almost thirty years.

In 1896 Victoria Park's supremacy as the local commercial amusement park was challenged by a competing new venture just west of it, on land held by the estate of George Monro.[12] Monro was a Toronto businessman and one-time mayor who had owned a large property at the eastern end of the district for decades. He died in 1878 but his estate retained this land and in 1896 leased the lakefront portion of it to the Toronto Railway Company. The TRC had been established a few years earlier, in 1891, by a group of Toronto capitalists intent on taking over the expiring contract and monopoly of the Toronto Street Railway, the horse-drawn tram service that had been serving the city since 1861. And it did as it intended, securing its own thirty-year contract to provide street railway service – on the condition that it electrify the system, something that street railways all over the world were doing in the 1890s.[13] The TRC leased this Monro estate land not for streetcars but for building and operating a new commercial amusement park, and in 1896 it opened what it called Munro Park – a name apparently already in local use for the property – employing the more conventional spelling of the family's name.[14]

Munro Park had something Victoria Park did not – copious electricity – because its owner had run electrical lines into the area to power its streetcars. (Owners of the Toronto Railway Company and the Toronto Electric Light Company, the city's main supplier of electricity, were closely allied.)[15] Victoria Park had installed some electric lights on its grounds the year before, using power it purchased from the TRC, but it could not compete with the street railway's own venture.[16] With its electricity Munro Park offered moving picture shows, indoor theatre, one of those giant, daring steel wheels with swinging benches that Mr. Ferris had devised for the 1893 Columbia Exhibition in Chicago, as well as an electric-powered merry-go-round that, to anyone who had ridden Victoria Park's steam-powered one, must have seemed nearly silent (figure 3). Victoria Park held out for a few years by scaling back its operations. But in 1900 the TRC, just prior to opening Munro Park for the season,

Figure 3. "Munro Park, Munro Park Avenue," c. 1900. A sunny day in Munro Park, with its Ferris wheel in clear view. The photographer, the photograph's origin, and its precise date are all unknown.

Courtesy of Toronto Public Library (PICTURES-R-5427)

took over Victoria Park's lease and incorporated the property into its own operations as a dancing-free picnic area, "thoroughly lighted thruout and placed under the strictest police supervisions."[17] Munro Park had bested its rival and would go on to several more years of successful operation.

***

City dwellers were beginning to affect the district in another way too, as more and more Toronto residents were finding the beach itself, and the lake, an attractive destination. Visitors were coming not just for the day but for weeks, in some cases entire summers, erecting cottages, boathouses, and tents of varying levels of permanence along the waterfront. The late-nineteenth-century cottaging fad, a phenomenon more commonly associated with Ontario's northern lakes, touched the shore of Lake Ontario too.[18]

Some early landowners or their lessees may have built seasonal cabins or cottages along the lake, but we know nothing of this, and the historical record is so slim we likely never will. The earliest patrician cottager we know something about is Sir Adam Wilson, a distinguished lawyer, politician, and ultimately chief justice of the Ontario Court of Queen's Bench, who was knighted upon his retirement in 1887 (figure 4; also see figure 2).[19] Wilson acquired a fifty-acre property in the eastern part of the district, south of the Kingston Road, in 1853, most of it from the creditors of William M. Gorrie, a local merchant and short-term owner of the property who must have somehow defaulted.[20] How and why Wilson came to own this extensive tract is something of a mystery. He seems not to have bought or sold any other major properties, so, unlike many of the district's other major landowners, he was not an active land speculator. One intriguing detail about his ownership is that for years the property was mortgaged to the estate of erstwhile Upper Canada Inspector General John Henry Dunn (d. 1854) – Wilson likely borrowed money from that estate to buy it, which would not have been unusual. Dunn's daughter Sophie was

Figure 4. "Sir Adam Wilson." A portrait – seemingly a photograph of a print – of Adam Wilson (not Sir until 1887) during his brief tenure as mayor (1859–60). It probably found its way to Quebec when Wilson was serving (1860–3) in the Legislative Assembly of the United Province of Canada, which was meeting those years in Quebec City. The portrait was later acquired and preserved by the City of Montreal Archives.

Courtesy of Archives de la Ville de Montréal (BM1-5P2250)

named in the sale of every piece of land that Wilson sold up until the late 1870s.[21]

In any case, Wilson's ownership was secure enough that at some point in the 1870s he built a summer home he called Balmy Beach cottage on level land beside a small stream just up from the beach, at what is now the foot of Willow Avenue.[22] No drawings, photographs, or descriptions of this structure are known to exist, and no physical vestiges remain (it was demolished in 1931), but from various sources we know its precise location and its footprint – some thirty or forty feet square – and that it was two storeys high with a partially bricked exterior and some sort of brick or stone basement, all of which reveal it to have been a substantial, rather permanent house.[23] How much time Wilson spent at it, we do not know. He lived in the city, on Spadina Avenue, more than ten kilometres away – at least an hour by horse and carriage – so as a busy man he could not have made the trip very often. He rented it out for the entire summer season in 1880, and perhaps other years too.[24] One biographical note states he came regularly only after he retired, in 1887; since he died in 1891 that would mean only four years of steady use.

We might not know how important Balmy Beach was to Judge Wilson, but we do know how important Judge Wilson was to Balmy Beach – not only as an early cottage owner but as a land developer of sorts as well. In January 1876 Wilson subdivided his entire tract into 149 large lots (136 feet wide and 287 feet deep) that were, a newspaper advertisement claimed, ideal for summer villas.[25] His plan of subdivision laid out a rectilinear grid of streets, all with

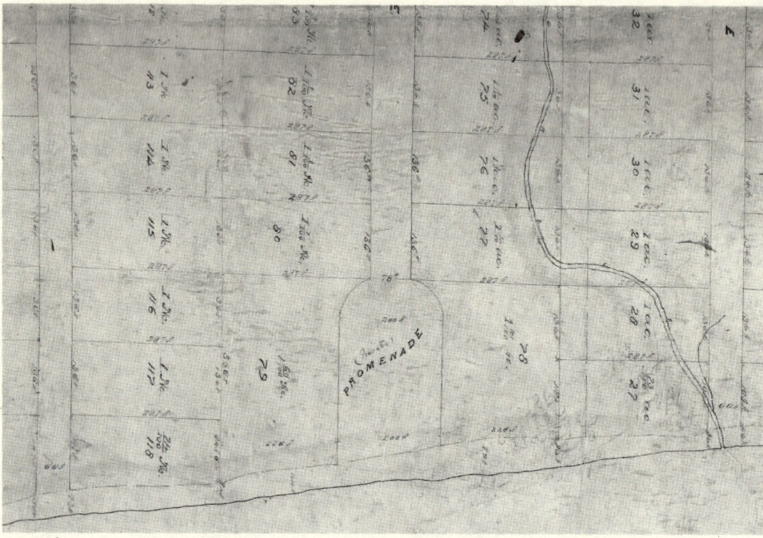

Figure 5. Lakefront portion of Adam Wilson's plan for his Balmy Beach subdivision, showing the central street (Beech Avenue) opening into a private lakefront promenade, the stream beside which Wilson built his cottage, and nineteen of the plan's 149 large (numbered) lots. This image has been extracted from a digitized copy of the original plan, drawn in coloured ink on linen.

Registered Plan of Subdivision #406, 17 January 1876 (Ontario Land Registry Holdings)

the names of trees, presumably to accentuate the natural setting and enhance its sales appeal. Beech Avenue was the central street, running north to south, and where it met the lake it widened into what the plan labelled a "(private) promenade," essentially a lakefront common for the subdivision's future residents (figure 5). How well Wilson had thought this through, or even how much of it was his own idea, we do not know as none of his personal papers relating to the undertaking have come to light. Semi-rural villa communities were cropping up around cities in many parts of the world in the late nineteenth century; *Villenkolonien*, or villa colonies, were especially common in German-speaking countries.[26] And exclusive park-like suburbs, designed by accomplished landscape architects, were being built near some major US cities – Riverside, outside Chicago, being the best known – although these were generally well beyond the urban edge, and for year-round living.[27] Wilson was worldly enough to have known of such places, but his Balmy Beach scheme, whatever prompted it, was so close to the city and so devoid of landscape design that it was unlikely to become one of them. And it never did. Few lots sold, and no community of villa owners ever appeared. Wilson died with little to show for his fifteen years as a property developer.

Yet his endeavour did not die with him. In 1880, a few years after registering his subdivision plan, Wilson brought four partners into his venture, each taking possession of a specific north-south strip of his land.[28] Orlando Winstanley (an English-trained medical doctor who had sold family landholdings in adjacent Scarborough Township some years earlier) was the first partner; in fact Wilson seems to have brought him in before registering his subdivision.[29] There was also James Beaty (a junior partner in Wilson's law firm who also owned land nearby in Scarborough Township), James's brother Robert Beaty (an entrepreneur with his own banking and brokerage firm), and Allan Maclean

Howard (an experienced property developer with holdings just west of Wilson's).[30] And after Wilson died these men followed through on his scheme. What they ultimately ended up creating, however, was not a villa community but a dense, middle-class residential suburb – a far cry from Wilson's vision (see chapter 3). But prior to 1900, before the suburb-building process took over, they and a few associates built their own substantial summer cottages along the waterfront, and in doing so spawned a small, short-lived recreational community bearing the name Balmy Beach.

Dr. Winstanley built the first cottage after Wilson's, in the early 1880s.[31] Winstanley seems to have been a restless, rather mercurial character and he soon sold off most of his holdings and moved away, leaving few traces of his involvement in Balmy Beach and no clear evidence of his cottage or where it stood. A rough sketch map drawn by a schoolchild in the 1930s, based on recollections recounted to her by a then-aged resident who grew up in the area in the 1880s, shows it west of the subdivision's central roadway – which would still have been just a sandy track – well back from the lake, but one should probably not take this placement too seriously.[32] A newspaper report from 1906 states that Winstanley's cottage was being used by the YMCA's Harriers' Club as its clubhouse. We know from multiple reliable sources that this clubhouse was at the eastern edge of the subdivision, on the lakefront, but we also know Winstanley never owned this property, so the claim that the Harriers' clubhouse was his cottage, though plausible, is questionable.[33] The location of Winstanley's Balmy Beach cottage will likely remain forever unknown.

The first assessment rolls for the district, which begin in 1889, record a substantial summer house on a large block of property comprising parts of lots 79, 116, 117, and 118 of Wilson's plan of subdivision, just west of the promenade.[34] There is no definitive record of who built this house, or when it was built, but signs point to it having been built for local entrepreneur Edward Trout and his wife, pioneer female physician Jenny Kidd Trout, probably about 1884. They are on record purchasing the land on which it stood in 1883 from the two Beaty brothers (for $5,339) – Wilson's 1880 division of land among his partners had allotted lot 79 to Robert and lots 116–18 to James.[35] Why the Trouts bought a plot comprising portions of four lots, rather than one single lot, we do not know. Perhaps it was an especially desirable site – drier, or more nicely treed – or perhaps a block of property laid out by a previous owner, prior to Wilson's subdivision, maybe with an old house still on it. But we have no evidence of any of this. All we have is a record, noted above, of it existing in 1889, and of the Trouts selling the entire property, house and land, that year for $10,500, suggesting major improvements over the years they had owned it (figure 6).[36] Its purchaser, John Leys, died in 1892 and his estate promptly put it up for sale, advertising it as a "valuable suburban residence" with the name "Fernwood."[37] The commercial grocer James Lumbers bought it from the Leys estate, and he used it often enough that it was soon known locally as his.[38] It must have been a substantial place. In August 1896 Mrs. Lumbers held

Figure 6: "Beech Avenue, at lakeshore, 1885." A photograph, of unknown origin, looking west along the bank at the foot of Beech Avenue, prior to any significant cottage-building. The bench, the white-painted flagpole behind it, and the stairway down to the lake (top step visible in lower left) – all indicating regular access by boat – were likely built in association with Fernwood. The spindly paper birch trees suggest land cleared decades earlier and left to regenerate.

Courtesy of Toronto Public Library (PICTURES-R-5455)

a garden party for their son's twenty-first birthday at which the guests "after enjoying themselves in the handsome, illuminated grounds adjourned to the residence where dancing, songs and recitations and light refreshments occupied their attention."[39]

By this time the Beaty brothers had taken action on the parts of their lakefront lots the Trouts had not bought. Robert Beaty built a substantial cottage of his own on the eastern part of his Lot 79, while James Beaty transferred the western portion of his Lots 116–18 to his daughter and her husband, A.J. Russell Snow, who, after further subdividing it in 1895, built a sizable family cottage on the lakefront lots his subdivision had created.[40] So by 1900 three substantial residences stood along the lake in the western half of the Balmy Beach subdivision – Robert Beaty's, Lumbers's, and Snow's. Though certainly not villas, they were good-sized summer homes. Snow's and Beaty's, whose footprints are on record (as of 1930), were both two-and-one-half-storey structures, some fifty feet square; they were entirely of wood, although Snow's, but not Beaty's, did have a basement foundation (see figure 31).[41] James Beaty erected a smaller cottage for himself on one of his lots north of Queen Street, well up from the lake, though he did not own it for long and he seems not to have used it much.

Nothing lasts long in property booms. By 1902 Lumbers had sold Fernwood to Emerson Coatsworth, a prominent single-term Conservative member of parliament (1891–6) who was already an active speculator in the area, and Coatsworth promptly subdivided the property into fourteen small lots, creating what he called the Fernwood Park subdivision.[42] The original house remained, spanning two of the new lots, though Coatsworth seems never to have lived in it and by 1906 had sold it.[43] Also in 1902 Allan Maclean Howard, the Balmy Beach partner holding the westernmost strip of Wilson's subdivision, further subdivided his villa-sized lakefront lot (#119) down to six smaller lots; Coatsworth obtained the most easterly of the lots and built a lakefront home on it.[44] The home was the largest of them all – just two storeys, but with a footprint bigger than Snow's or Beaty's (figure 7).

Figure 7. A lakefront cottage, built c. 1900, west side of Balsam Avenue at the beach, initially owned and occupied by, and probably built for, Emerson Coatsworth. The photograph (looking northwest) was taken by the Assessment Department in September 1930 in preparation for its expropriation and demolition (see chapter 6).

City of Toronto Archives (Series 372, Sub-series 3, Item 390)

A similar pattern emerged east along the lake. The lakefront property immediately east of the promenade, Lot 78, was in Winstanley's strip of land.[45] Winstanley seems to have had trouble holding onto his Balmy Beach lots. He may have been under financial strain, for he sold some quite early on, before the other partners did, and records show him transferring many of them to and from his son and wife through the 1880s. Then in 1890 he sold this lakefront lot to Catherine H. Barnett, an associate of Wilson's about whom little has come to light, and she subdivided it into four lots, which she sold.[46] The first two buyers put up good-sized wooden cottages – Dr. Winstanley's daughter Ada and her husband, A.J.W. McMichael, were the first – although the latter two buyers built smaller, more conventional city homes.[47] Wilson's own original cottage stood further east, on Lot 27, the lakefront of the strip of land he had kept for himself.[48] He sold this lot along with many others (see chapter 3) to Barnett in 1890, just before he died, but she left his cottage intact. So by 1900 a short run of good-sized summer homes stood along the Balmy Beach lakefront on both sides of the promenade.

Grand lakefront homes, however, were not what these entrepreneurial landowners had in mind for their properties. Snow, Coatsworth, and Howard had by now subdivided all their lakefront land into conventionally sized urban lots, no doubt expecting buyers to erect conventionally sized urban houses on them, and that is indeed what happened. Snow had used all three of his lakefront lots for his own cottage, giving him some open space either side of it, but every lakefront lot in Coatsworth's and Howard's subdivisions soon had a house on it. These were beach houses in a sense, for they faced the lake, and several had boathouses in front of them, but they were built nearly lot line to lot line and looked more urban than rural.[49] The partners were beginning to sell lots away from the lake, too, facing the streets of the subdivision. Most of these were in the block just north of the lake, but some were on the upper plain, far from the beach.[50] It is hard to call these "cottages." Some, such as Charles T. Whatmough's and James E. Snider's, built within a few years of each other around 1900 on the upper plain along Beech Avenue north of Pine, in Winstanley's tract, might have been used only seasonally at first, but being oriented towards the street, far from the lake, and quite substantial, "cottage" is not the word, and the owners did soon occupy them year-round.[51] Others, such as accountant Frederick W. Robarts's substantial home on Balsam Avenue just up from the lake and William J. Gardiner's smaller place further up Balsam Avenue, looked like cottages but were in fact year-round family homes.[52]

So Balmy Beach was transitioning into a residential suburb, but in 1900 the process had only begun. Most of the lakefront houses, notwithstanding their urban form, did function as beach houses – the boathouses make that clear enough (figure 8).[53] Rental accommodation for recreational visitors was still on offer. Many shops and services were still seasonal, notably an unusual "tent church" that held well-attended services two evenings a week throughout the summer.[54] The land was still mostly brush and forest – building lots seem to have been cleared only after they were purchased – and roads were still little more than sandy trails. The Balmy Beach community applied for a post office in 1899, stating its population as 150 families.[55] How many of these were cottagers, in the sense of seasonal residents, one cannot say, but the community's social life still revolved around recreation, and even year-round residents, the children and young adults at least, made regular use of the lake and the beach in the summer. This colony of middle-class, or perhaps at this point upper-middle-class, recreationists was surely not what Judge Wilson had envisioned, but, who knows, maybe he would have approved.

Figure 8. Private houses, with private boat houses, along the Balmy Beach lakefront between Balsam and Fernwood Park Avenues, built c. 1900 and photographed 1931, shortly before their demolition. All three – one detached (#328) and two semi-detached (#330 and #332) – look more like city houses than lakefront cottages. (In the absence of an actual street, houses on the lake were given addresses on Lake Front.)

City of Toronto Archives (Series 372, Sub-series 3, Item 1180)

***

A similar phenomenon was underway a kilometre west at Kew Beach, the name by then being applied to the beach either side of, and to some extent in front of, Kew Gardens. Its development as a recreational area had begun a little earlier than Balmy Beach's. Soon after Joseph Williams opened Kew Gardens, in 1879, he began leasing lakefront lots – though he filed no plans of subdivision – on which his lessees erected cottages.[56] But the Kew Beach community encompassed more than Williams's family holdings. In 1885 a market gardener named Justus Dunn, who owned lakefront property just east of Kew Gardens – a rare farmer landowner – subdivided his land into about a dozen small lots on which buyers built small cottages.[57] Dunn's subdivision was entirely beach-oriented; the north-south road bisecting it, which was not a public road, did not extend north to intersect any city street. At about the same time the owner of the land west of Kew Gardens, Joseph L. Thompson, subdivided his entire tract from the lake to Queen Street and in doing so created a run of beach-facing lots across the south end of his property.[58] These lakefront lots sold steadily through the 1890s. With no bank or cliff along this part of the lake, these were true beachfront lots. Their front yards were sand.

The lessees and buyers of these lots look to have been a mix of builders hoping to sell what they built, commercial owners planning to rent what they built, and individuals intending to live in what they built, and it is hard to determine which predominated. What is evident, however, is that the houses on Thompson's lots were squeezed in two, or even three, to a lot. The corporate owner of the westernmost part of the district, the Scottish Ontario and Manitoba Land Company, had created no beachfront lots when it subdivided its holdings in the 1880s, probably because the southern portion of its land was marshy.[59] But when Emerson Coatsworth acquired that land in 1901, he promptly subdivided it into small beach-facing lots, all of which were soon crammed with houses as well.[60]

The upshot was that by shortly after 1900 the half-kilometre of beach from Woodbine Avenue to beyond Kew Gardens was a nearly continuous run of private structures on lots often fifteen or twenty feet wide.[61] It presented quite a pot-pourri of designs – if one can even apply that word – with buildings ranging from shacks to substantial houses. Many of the latter would not have looked out of place on adjacent residential streets – perhaps they were built by the same builders – though most did have a second-floor porch or balcony that acknowledged the beach (figure 9). Nearly all were of wood, most lacked foundations, and their assessed values, from just $200 to $500, reflected this.[62] They tended to be owned by individuals, although since several owners owned more than one house a good proportion of residents were tenants. Several members of the Williams family still leased and rented out properties in front of, and increasingly east of, their Kew Gardens land.[63]

Signs of permanent settlement were emerging here too, as at Balmy Beach: residential development was edging up from the lake on both sides of Kew Gardens, a fledgling public school and volunteer fire company had been formed, and several small churches had appeared. Kew Beach petitioned for its post office in 1896, stating a population of 250 families.[64] Yet it was still, again like Balmy Beach, primarily a lake-oriented recreational community.

But it was a different sort of recreational community. Unlike Balmy Beachers, Kew Beachers appear to have had no sense of their exclusivity; the community's name, after all, had been bestowed on it by an entrepreneurial farmer, not a knighted judge who lived off the public purse, and much

Figure 9. Houses facing Kew Beach, built c. 1900, photographed 1930, demolished 1931. The two houses, addressed as 96 and 98 Lake Front, were on a single lot; they were built entirely of wood and lacked basement foundations. The Lombardy poplars – fast-growing non-native trees – were likely planted by the initial owners in search of a little shade.

City of Toronto Archives (Series 372, Sub-series 3, Item 813)

of its waterfront land was being sold or leased by that farmer's family, not by barristers, financiers, or future mayors.[65] Nearly all its cottages were quite modest; the one striking exception was the cottage of James Gunn, senior manager of the street railway; it faced the beach on the west side of Lee Avenue and was reportedly large enough for small non-denominational church services.[66] Kew Beach was, in other words, more "popular." In 1898 *Toronto World* reported that some 1,500 people had spent Dominion (Canada) Day at Kew Beach, with revellers lingering around a bonfire until midnight.[67] Balmy Beach was not that kind of place. Later the same summer a group of Balmy Beach cottagers hosted a garden-party fundraiser in their waterfront promenade for the newly formed Fresh Air Fund. Their park was "gaily decorated with hundreds of lanterns" and the Queen's Own Band performed. Some 2,000 people attended – by invitation.[68] Even more telling, the previous summer a number of Balmy Beach residents had assembled on Queen Street in the dark of night to unstack and scatter a load of rails the street railway had brought in to extend its line to Munro Park, a noisy, irksome place that they thought should be made harder, not easier, to get to.[69]

***

The beach scene blossomed further after 1900, at both locations. Residents of Balmy and Kew Beach formed athletic/social clubs with memberships and resources sufficient to build lakefront clubhouses for social gatherings and sporting competitions, of which there were many.[70] Social columns in Toronto newspapers regularly reported from both communities. These columns relate that in mid-August 1903 seventy-five people attended a Balmy Beach Club dance at the firehall, there being no clubhouse yet ("Mrs. Ramsay at the piano played in excellent time"), and that eighteen tables participated in a euchre night at the Kew Beach clubhouse ("Miss Chalieu was awarded a prize for least games won").[71] Nearly every lakefront lot was now built on, and at least one new tourist hotel, The Pines, opened in Balmy Beach.[72] Dozens of small summer cottages were now being erected on Woodbine Beach, the city-owned sandspit curving into the lake at the western end of the district.[73]

Yet beneath all this good fun was the inescapable reality that the entire district was becoming more closely linked to Toronto, which by 1900 was a metropolis of some 200,000 expanding more rapidly than ever. A generation earlier, in 1880, the County of York had finally made the track running east from the Kingston Road turnoff into a proper road through to the York/Scarborough Township line (present-day Victoria Park Avenue), and the name Queen Street began being applied to its entire length. Development soon followed on either side of the street and in 1887 the City of Toronto annexed the roadway and began improving the road itself and building sidewalks alongside it. This annexation obliged the Toronto Street Railway to extend its service into the neighbourhood, which it did in 1889, though only as far as Lee Avenue; the newly formed Toronto Railway Company electrified that line in May 1893, and a month later extended it the five hundred or so metres to the city boundary at Maclean Avenue once the City filled the wetland and graded Queen Street to its satisfaction.[74] Cars went no further however because land east of Maclean was in the municipality of East Toronto (incorporated in 1888) and the TRC, lacking a contract with East Toronto, could not run into its jurisdiction. The company found this especially bothersome after it opened Munro Park in 1896 and wished to convey park visitors directly to the entrance. This was resolved in 1898, and the company soon had electric streetcar service running through the entire Beaches district – notwithstanding the Balmy Beachers' act of resistance noted above.

Closer connections to Toronto brought more year-round residents, signs of which would have been hard to miss. Christian congregations built more substantial churches, Presbyterians and Baptists being the first to take this step.[75] The City built a fine new firehall and the Toronto School Board built a more permanent public school, both to serve Kew Beach. Electricity and telephone companies erected poles and strung wires alongside the streets. New owners cleared lots and constructed houses – indeed one journalist reported a "building boom" in the Balmy Beach area in 1899, with eighteen permanent houses of various sizes under construction at the time of writing.[76] Yet as visible as this all must have been, and as boisterous as Balmy and Kew beaches surely were on warm summer days, the population of the district remained low. An eighteen-house building boom produced plenty of hammer noise, but it was not a demographic event. Overall population counts were not done but numbers remained in the hundreds. In 1900 a Toronto journalist reported – how accurately we cannot assess – 287 houses in the entire Beaches district (sixty-five facing the lake) of which just ninety-two were lived in year-round.[77] Those numbers were rising, but the district was not yet a city neighbourhood.

CHAPTER THREE

Suburb Building

The pre-1900 pattern of development based on the appeal of the lake would not last. Beginning in the 1880s, increasingly in the 1890s, and more rapidly still once full electric street railway service was introduced, a more conventional suburb-building process – already underway closer to the city – gained momentum, and by 1900 had taken hold. One by one the area's patrician property owners, aware that the strong demand for housing was increasing the value of local land, subdivided their holdings (or in some cases sold their property intact to a more active speculator who did so) and sold the resulting lots to builders who erected houses to sell to a growing number of willing buyers. The lake and the beach, raisons d'être of early development, became little more than the southern limit of saleable residential property.

There was no plan, and public authorities exerted little control over what was built.[1] The streets of one property owner's subdivision might or might not line up with those of an adjacent owner. Roads were straight and at right angles to one another because there was no reason to curve or angle them, and because it made the lots – all platted square to the street – easier to measure and draw.[2] Lot sizes were determined not by any planner or public agent but by the subdividers and their surveyors; most lots were small, for modest homes – potential buyers were far from affluent – but some were larger, for larger homes. There were no regulations prescribing where certain land uses should or should not go, how much or what land should be used as public space, or that streets should be designed to suit their function – Queen Street, clearly the neighbourhood's *rue principale*, was one survey chain (66 feet) wide, like all standard Ontario roads.[3] The form of this emerging suburb, in short, reflected the wishes of its landowners; as an observer of comparable suburb building in Montreal once noted, "the speculative owner of property rules the day."[4]

That is not to say the process was entirely free of government oversight. Ontario law required that any owner intending to subdivide property had to register a "plan of subdivision" with the provincial land registry before proceeding. These plans, to be drawn by provincially certified surveyors, had to show the precise dimensions of all newly created lots and streets and assign numbers to the lots and names to the streets. Once formally "registered," a plan of subdivision became the document of record for the property.[5] But the registry office demanded nothing more than information. There was no broader plan into which individual plans had to fit; nor were these plans "reviewed" or "approved" as they are today. The purpose of registration was to put on record what property owners did, not to control what they did. Only with the enactment of provincial planning legislation in 1912 did public authorities gain some say over the subdivision process and over how subdivided land would be used, and not until 1914 did the City begin to enforce "building lines" that regulated setbacks on residential streets.[6] Roads were subject to somewhat more control. The Municipal Act (not the Registry Act) stipulated that city streets be at least sixty-six feet wide, although it also stated that a subdivider could disregard this requirement if it had "the consent of the council of the municipality," and this consent seems to have been easy enough to obtain.[7]

This lack of regulation was not unusual in the Anglo world. London, England, had been growing this way for centuries, as its bewildering array of present-day streets reveals. By the late nineteenth century, however, the notion that some overarching authority could and probably should shape urban expansions had begun gaining adherents. The Garden City movement underway in Britain at this time rested on the idea that an entire city could be conceived and built in a prescribed manner, and such thinking was also being applied to garden suburbs at a city's edge. Even more directly applicable was the German concept of comprehensive town extension planning in which peripheral urban expansion was prescribed to ensure a pleasing and functional design of all newly urbanized areas. (figure 10). This idea, being applied in Vienna among other places in the German-speaking world, was drawing international attention in the very years that the Beaches began

Figure 10. "Berlin. Reichskanzlerplatz, im Hintergrund die Heerstraße im Bau," 1907, photograph by Waldemar Franz Hermann Titzenthaler. A planned urban extension west of Berlin, with the main road, public gardens, electric lighting, and the U-bahn – note the entrances – all in place prior to full development. Reichskanzlerplatz has undergone several name changes since its creation. It is now Theodor-Heuss-Platz.

Public domain, Wikimedia Commons

to be built.[8] But one suspects most Toronto city councillors and builders knew as much about Viennese city-building as they knew about Sigmund Freud.

The first significant act of subdivision had been done much earlier, by Adam Wilson, when he created the Balmy Beach subdivision in the eastern end of the district. A small recreational community had emerged in the southern portion of his subdivision by the 1890s, but by then Wilson's partners had also begun selling residential lots well away from the lake, and in doing so had started the process of turning Balmy Beach into a residential suburb.

Their first step was to further subdivide, or "sub-subdivide," Wilson's villa-sized (136-foot-wide) lots down to a smaller, more saleable, width, usually fifty feet. This might have been their intention when they first joined Wilson's scheme in 1880, but certainly by the 1890s, with scant demand for villa-sized lots, they had no realistic alternative.[9] In some cases, they brought in partners when they did their sub-subdividing, perhaps to assist with the not insignificant costs of surveying, advertising the lots, and perhaps doing some preliminary roadbuilding. The Beaty brothers, in 1895, had sub-subdivided a jointly owned tract of twenty villa-sized lots north of Queen Street into over a hundred fifty-foot lots, and for this had brought in a third partner (only five lots had houses on them in 1900). Allan Maclean Howard brought in multiple partners when he sub-subdivided some of his Balmy Beach land south of Queen Street.[10]

At times Wilson and his partners sold tracts of villa-sized lots to others who then carried out the further subdividing. Two of their earliest sales, in the 1880s, worked this way. In one case, in 1886, Winstanley sold ten of his lots on the hill north of Queen Street to future mayor (and future street railway executive) Robert J. Fleming in partnership with Emerson Coatsworth, also a future mayor, and the buyers did the further subdividing; their plan created an unusual pattern, its eastern half being laid out in long, narrow north-south oriented lots.[11] In the other, Wilson sold seven lots in the easternmost strip of the subdivision, which he had kept for himself, to a partnership of small builders who further subdivided it into eleven still fairly large square lots, creating Glen Fern and Balmy Avenues.[12] It would be some twenty years before most of the lots created in these transactions saw any building, over which time some were resold more than once. In 1890, the year before he died, Wilson sold what remained of his personal holdings to speculators/builders. He sold seven villa-sized lots to Catherine Barnett, including the lakefront site of his own cottage, mentioned above, and she, in partnership with Wilson, further subdivided them into twenty-five smaller lots along Silver Birch Avenue.[13] At about the same time Wilson sold nearly all his property north of Queen Street, more than forty villa-sized lots in all, to a builder named Arthur Wellington Burk, who further subdivided them.[14]

By the mid-1890s, much of Balmy Beach had been sub-subdivided and the next step, selling the lots, had begun. Owners sold either to commercial builders or to individuals wanting to build their own home, or, in what looks to have been a common combination of the two, to commercial builders who bought a short run of lots, built a home for themselves on one and then built a few more, to sell or rent, on the others. Most building lots were fifty feet wide, though some were smaller, and on many of them builders erected two houses, and in a few cases even two pairs of "semi-detached" houses – four separate residences. Nothing required builders to do this, but neither did anything prohibit it. Builders were simply responding to the market: if small houses sold better than large houses, builders built small houses. Small houses would also have been easier and faster to build, so building them was a sound strategy for a small-scale entrepreneur with limited capital. This act of squeezing multiple small houses into sub-subdivided lots was debasing Wilson's vision for Balmy Beach, no doubt, but there was no stopping it.[15]

Balmy Beach's beginnings as a villa colony, fanciful though that turned out to be, did leave behind a few eccentricities. Rather surprisingly, the provincial law requiring plans of subdivision did not require that large lots be formally sub-subdivided for multiple houses to be built on them.[16] Buyers could simply obtain title to a defined portion of a lot and build on that portion, with the original plan of subdivision remaining the plan of record. The Balmy Beach partner who made greatest use of this was Allan Maclean Howard, owner of the westernmost strip. Howard registered no plans of sub-subdivision for any of his villa-sized lots until 1900, yet he began building on Balsam Avenue south of Queen Street before 1900, simply putting more than one house on each of the lots.[17] He kept this up north of Queen too, after 1900, where in fact he never sub-subdivided the villa-sized lots. Most houses were built there three to a 136-foot lot, so the lack of sub-subdividing did not produce a density lower than where builders were putting one house on a fifty-foot lot. But houses built on Howard's lots were all detached, generally larger and of better quality than houses elsewhere, and many were of brick, not yet common in Balmy Beach. It seems that Howard took Adam Wilson's vision of an exclusive community more to heart than the other partners, and believed that retaining the original large lots would help him do so. But owners/builders left a few villa-sized lots unsubdivided in other places too – notably in what was originally Winstanley's strip of land in the centre of the subdivision – and these lots also often had larger houses built on them. Villa-sized lots were left intact on Beech Avenue, north of Pine Avenue and south of Queen Street, and are recognizable to this day by their large houses with deep front setbacks.[18] Vestiges of Wilson's vision remained on the Balmy Beach landscape.

Other Balmy Beach eccentricities are due to the area having been built with minimal municipal oversight. Cities did not control the platting of subdivisions, as noted, although they did have some say over the structural integrity of buildings and the width of streets.[19] But the original subdivision (1876) and the first sub-subdivisions (1887) were done with no municipal oversight whatsoever because the town of East Toronto was not incorporated until 1888, and even after the town was formed it seems to have been disinclined to impose on its major property owners – who might well have been town councillors. This lack of oversight resulted in some unusually narrow streets, unconventional lot arrangements, and precariously graded hillside lots.[20] The most extreme example of this might be Sycamore Avenue; laid out as a thirty-three-foot-wide lane in the Beaty brothers' 1895 plan of subdivision, it was somehow developed ten years later as a thirty-three-foot-wide residential street.[21]

Why Wilson's Balmy Beach subdivision had been included within East Toronto when that town's principal raison d'être was the Grand Trunk Railway depot and yard, well north of the Beaches, we do not know. Balmy Beach had next to no functional or social linkages to the rest of East Toronto; indeed, in 1900 nearly half the residents of East Toronto north of Kingston Road worked for the GTR – the town was almost an industrial suburb – while not one East Toronto resident living south of Kingston Road, in Balmy Beach, worked for the GTR.[22] But whatever the reason, Balmy Beach was part of East Toronto, and after about 1900 the town began providing the subdivision with municipal services, building a school, a small waterworks, and a fire-hall to serve the area.[23]

Some residents of Balmy Beach, however, held firm to the notion of their community being a distinct, rather exclusive place, and they had enough sway on East Toronto council to ensure that municipal actions accorded with that notion. But East Toronto council was not going to survive the town's annexation by the City of Toronto, negotiations for which were underway in 1908, and the council's dissolution would leave Balmy Beach with no means of controlling its destiny. How much clout would Balmy Beach have on *Toronto* city council? So in a final effort to preserve the community's special identity, East Toronto council demanded that the terms of annexation designate Balmy Beach "a residential district, free from factories and hotels," and the City of Toronto acceded to this. It was a curious restriction, for there is no sign that anyone wanted to build factories – where would they go? – and the area already had hotels, but it was put in place nonetheless, presumably with an eye to the future.[24] And at the time railway companies were thought to be considering running lines through the neighbourhood – wetlands and steep hills no longer being the impediment they were in 1850 – so residents were understandably on guard.[25]

Balmy Beach's unusual genesis also contributed to the survival, in altered form, of Wilson's waterfront promenade. Wilson had designated it as a private community space and named two of his partners as its trustees. The trustees upheld this designation, although the trusteeships themselves changed hands as the trustees sold out or died. In 1903 with the area clearly diverging from Wilson's vision, the last surviving trustee donated the promenade to the municipality of East Toronto for use as a public park. This donation, enacted by provincial legislation, included some unusual terms.[26] The park was to be exclusively for residents of East Toronto (no longer just for residents of the Balmy Beach subdivision) and their guests, which is to say that anyone living west of Maclean Avenue, a few blocks west of the park, or any visitors to the local commercial amusement park, could not, strictly speaking, enter unless brought in by a local. Furthermore, since the small town of East Toronto did not have a parks department, the terms gave its town council the authority to appoint a "Board of Management of Balmy Beach Park," consisting only of local residents, to set and enforce park policies.

It so happened that the Balmy Beach Club was being established at about this time, and the club's board of directors obtained permission from the park's board of management – the two bodies would have had common interests, and maybe common members – to build their private clubhouse in this public park. Then when East Toronto was annexed, its council demanded, and again Toronto agreed, that Balmy

Beach Park not be made a City of Toronto park; had it become a Toronto park the private club's occupation of the public space would likely have come to an end.[27] This anomaly prevails to this day. The private Balmy Beach clubhouse – not the original, which burned down – and its large parking lot still occupy most of public Balmy Beach Park, a curious vestige of localism and exclusivity.

***

The subdivision process was well underway in other parts of the district too. The westernmost tract – the western half of Lot 5 in the original colonial survey – had by this time been acquired by the Glasgow-based Scottish Manitoba and Ontario Land Company, a firm with hundreds of shareholders, most in Scotland but a few dozen in Toronto.[28] It filed a plan of subdivision in 1885, creating dozens of hundred-foot-wide lots, large enough for multiple houses, along a street south of Queen Street it named Kippendavie – an ancient site in Scotland – and several short streets north of Queen.[29] The land immediately east of this, the eastern half of Lot 5, had been owned since at least 1853, and likely earlier, by the successful and very well-connected Scottish-born builder John Ewart (1788–1856) and later by his estate.[30] Joseph L. Thompson had acquired the southern portion of it, from Queen Street south to the lake in the early 1880s, and he soon subdivided it into 118 fifty-foot lots, creating Kenilworth Avenue and Waverley Road, while a new owner of the northern portion, name illegible, did the same north of Queen, extending Waverley Road up to Kingston Road with fifty-foot lots but leaving the western half of his holding unsubdivided on account of a troublesome creek.[31]

Property east of this, Lot 4 in the original survey, had been subdivided decades earlier by its owner, Martin Peter Hayes, into park lots – large, semi-rural lots often used as an intermediate step in the development process – bisected with a road allowance (later Lee Avenue).[32] By 1860 Hayes had sold these lots, in separate parcels to different individuals, and most of them seem to have been resold at least once in the following decades. One parcel was the large block of lakefront land Joseph Williams acquired in 1854 and turned into Kew Gardens in 1879. At some point in the 1880s a parcel south of Queen Street, along the east side of Kew Gardens down to the lake, had been acquired by Walter S. Lee, a local financier and property developer well connected in civic affairs.[33] Lee kept all his land in park lots through the 1890s. The western half of the former Hayes property north of Kew Gardens, however, was subdivided into fifty-foot building lots in 1889 in two separate plans of subdivision by two separate owners. These latter two acts of subdivision, which laid out Wheeler and Bellefair Avenues, were particularly fanciful since the northern portion of those subdivisions was traversed by two substantial streams, each with associated hills and vales, making sale and development of lots there most unlikely (figure 11).[34]

Further east still, north of Queen, between the district's major ravine and the Balmy Beach subdivision, was land that Allan Maclean Howard (b. 1825) had owned prior to buying into Wilson's Balmy Beach undertaking.[35] At some point around 1890, Howard brought his son of the same name (b. 1852) into the business. Father and son had identical jobs too, Clerk at the

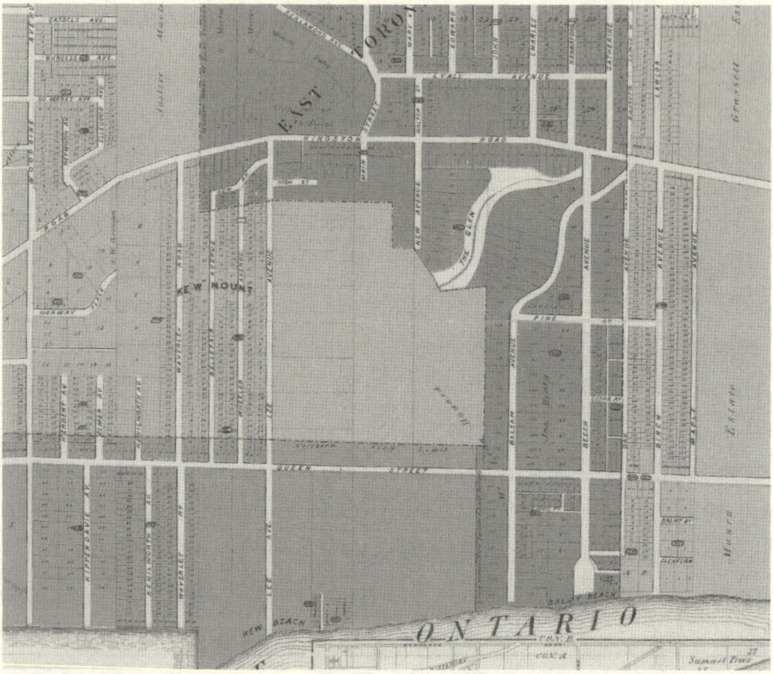

Figure 11. Registered subdivisions c. 1895 (mid-grey indicates City of Toronto, dark grey East Toronto, light grey unincorporated land in York Township). In Balmy Beach, some villa-size lots remain, but "sub-subdivision" was nearly complete in the eastern portion. The small block of lots beside "Kew Beach" is the stand-alone Leuty Avenue subdivision. The name Kew Mount for the higher ground in the west, north of Queen Street, never caught on.

City of Toronto Archives (Series 726, Item 514)

York County First Division Court, so references to them can be confusing, but they both seem to have been involved in selling their Balmy Beach property, south of Queen, along a street they had named Howard Avenue.[36] One wonders how they managed to hold presumably full-time, salaried jobs while working actively as property developers – were their jobs mere sinecures? – although one also suspects that their positions connected them with prospective buyers. The Howards look to have been very good at what they did, successfully employing the technique of selling multiple lots to builders, who then built and sold, or rented out, what they built – a strategy that would have freed up their capital and effectively transferred future risk to the builders.[37] After 1900 they began developing their holdings north of Queen Street, both within and west of Balmy Beach, starting with the younger Howard erecting his own home on Queen Street, outside Balmy Beach proper, in 1902. His house was notable for being architect-designed and unambiguously year-round, as well as for the ducks and geese he kept on the large stream-fed pond that had formed in the low land west of the house after Queen Street was filled and graded for the streetcar in 1893 (figure 12).[38]

Subdividing picked up steam after 1900, with the entire neighbourhood now served by the street railway. Walter S. Lee began subdividing his land south of Queen before he died in 1902, and his heir completed the job after his death.[39] North of Queen Street the undeveloped property east of Lee Avenue was subdivided and built on, one portion by financier and city councillor W.J. Hambly, who gave his name to a street, and another by Joseph Williams, who bestowed more London on the neighbourhood by creating Hammersmith and Islesworth

COTTAGE FOR A. McLEAN HOWARD, EAST TORONTO.
C. F. WAGNER, ARCHITECT, TORONTO.

Figure 12. Allan Maclean Howard Jr.'s new house (upper) on the north side of Queen Street, built 1902, and a 1920 view of the large pond he maintained just west of the house. This bucolic vista charmed passing pedestrians for several decades.

Courtesy of Toronto Public Library. Upper: Baldwin Collection, "Toronto Architectural Eighteen Club Catalogue," 1902, p. 37; Lower: LOCHIST-BE-096

Avenues on land he had purchased in 1871.[40] West of there, lots along Wheeler, Bellefair, and Waverley saw changes of ownership and further subdivision, although only the dry, southern portions attracted buyers at first, and Kenilworth Avenue was rather awkwardly extended both into and above the creek bed, making some oddly configured and highly flood-prone lots.[41] And in the east end, beyond Balmy Beach, when the Toronto Railway Company gave up its lease and shut down Munro Park in 1907, the managers of George Monro's estate hastily subdivided the property, creating the streets of Neville Park and Munro Park.[42] By about 1910, except for two large blocks of land (development of which is recounted in chapter 5), the subdivision of land into building lots was essentially complete.

***

Subdividing land does not mean building houses, but in these prewar boom years it might as well have. Demand for housing was so strong that, aside from a few problematic sites, the latter followed the former almost as night follows day. By 1913, the first year for which commercial fire insurance maps show individual buildings in the Beaches – itself a telling fact – most subdivided lots had houses on them.[43] The major exceptions were lots in the northwest part of the neighbourhood, where much of the terrain was hilly and swampy, and those on the Munro estate in the southeast, which had been subdivided only in 1907, although even it was already about half built. By rough count, the neighbourhood in 1913 contained upwards of 800 houses.[44] Neighbourhood population figures were not recorded, or if they were the records have been lost, and house counts are an imprecise indicator since an unknown number of new houses were still vacant, but all things considered, and with Toronto households in 1901 consisting of, on average, five people, the neighbourhood's 1913 year-round population would have been in the thousands.[45]

The housing varied in size and quality, and correspondingly in price.[46] This new residential suburb was by no means uniformly affluent, a quality that the word "suburb" still connotes in some minds. There were substantial houses, for sure, especially along Balsam Avenue and in the newest subdivisions at the neighbourhood's extreme east end. But for every solid brick home or grand but aging summer cottage there was at least one side-by-side duplex or lakefront shack. This diversity of housing, one might note, was entirely a product of free enterprise; potential homebuyers ranged from lower-middle to upper-middle class, so builders built a corresponding range of house sizes. Also noteworthy is that a degree of spatial differentiation of house quality was emerging. Small, lower value, wooden-framed houses were more common in the west, while larger, higher-value houses, some built of or clad in brick, were more common in the east (figure 13). This generalization requires a caveat: higher value houses were by no means absent in the west, were beginning to appear in the centre, and were not everywhere in the east. Around the corner from a run of substantial homes in the Balmy Beach area were some of the smallest lots and meanest houses in the district, notably the dense subdivision that Emerson Coatsworth had carved out of the old Fernwood estate west of the Balmy Beach promenade. But that said, a modest degree of east-west difference had developed.

Figure 13. Housing in the east (upper), on Munro Park Avenue, built 1913, one house per lot, the first permanent occupant a "manufacturer's agent," and in the west, on Kenilworth Avenue, built 1905 (on left) and 1908, two houses per lot, occupants of both changed frequently, among them a foreman, a carpenter, a grocer, a shoemaker, and a driver.

City of Toronto Archives (Series 372, Sub-series 3, Items 149 (upper) and 788)

Why it developed is hard to say. It was at least partly a manifestation of the social difference between the Balmy and Kew Beach recreational communities, which itself was a vestige of Adam Wilson's vision of Balmy Beach. It may also have been for more practical reasons – portions of land in the west were swampy and thus less valuable. Chronology could also have been a factor. Year-round houses began being built in the west in the 1890s, when streetcar service to the neighbourhood was still infrequent, and perhaps that prompted builders to build houses for those who could not afford to live in better-served locations.[47] This last reason only goes so far, however, for builders continued building small, wooden-clad houses in the Kew Beach area – Waverley, Kenilworth, and Kippendavie – even after full streetcar service was in place. Streetcar service was certainly not the sole determinant of housing quality in this streetcar suburb – clearly other factors were at work (see chapter 4) – but it, especially frequent service, is correlated with the construction of higher-value houses everywhere in the neighbourhood.[48]

It is worth emphasizing, however, that quite apart from any impact the streetcar might or might not have had on housing quality, it was still at the heart of the neighbourhood's genesis. The Beaches was unmistakably a streetcar suburb. Employment in Edwardian Toronto was strongly centralized, with jobs of all types – commercial, administrative, and even industrial – concentrated in the central city, so going to work meant travelling downtown. Of 261 Beaches residents whose employment location was identified in this study, 240 (92 per cent) worked downtown.[49] With every household needing at least one gainfully employed person, there being no "idle rich" among this first generation of suburban settlers and next to no social assistance, a good portion of the neighbourhood population made a trip to and from downtown every day. And since the only means of doing so was the Queen Street streetcar – walking being unrealistic for such a distance – going to work for Beaches residents meant riding the streetcar. There was simply no alternative in the pre-automobile age. Had there been no streetcar, there would have been no suburb.

Another important aspect of the neighbourhood's early housing is that it was built with almost no input from professional architects or designers. With very few exceptions, houses were "designed" by the builders who built them. Moreover, since most builders worked on a small scale, with the means to construct only a few houses, scores of builders contributed to the neighbourhood's creation, each with their own tastes and skills and social affinity. The upshot was a stylistic diversity of sorts; Beaches streetscapes often included a few nearly identical houses by one builder alongside another few nearly identical houses by another builder. Yet this diversity was strictly constrained by the conventions of the day and the preferences of buyers, so the housing actually had a certain sameness about it. How could it not? Small-scale speculative builders must think more about sales potential than design innovation. If Toronto's emerging home-owning class wanted houses that faced the street, had a small shingle-style front gable, a porch with faux-classical columns, and a few Victorian decorations, and you could build such houses cheaply but solidly, why build anything else?[50] This was especially sensible if the builder up the street had just done so and sold every house he built.

Some sixty years ago, the American historian Sam Bass Warner, in a now-classic book on Boston's streetcar suburbs, undertook to identify who built the houses in his study area, where the builders came from, and when and how they acquired their skills. Warner discovered that literally hundreds of local builders had built the houses and that most of them built only a few, often adjacent to their own. He learned that much of the inspiration for their house designs came from what had already been built (and sold) nearby,[51] and that these builders, mostly self-taught rather than formally trained tradesmen, typically came from the country or small towns. This last observation led him to assert that, whereas the townhouses and commercial buildings of early American cities had mimicked those of London or Paris, "the new streetcar suburbs looked like an enormous proliferation of the small town."[52] While research for this study has not been as exhaustive as that done by Warner, it has been sufficient to suggest that what occurred in Toronto's Beaches neighbourhood closely parallels what happened in Warner's Boston neighbourhoods. Particularly in the earlier-built streets in the western portion, the Beaches does indeed resemble "an enormous proliferation of the small town."

This absence of professional input pertains to the physical neighbourhood generally, not just to its houses. The neighbourhood certainly was not planned, in any sense of the word. Planned residential neighbourhoods were not common in North American cities in 1900, but they were not unheard of, even in Toronto. The Lawrence Park garden suburb in North Toronto, for example, had been fully planned by 1913.[53] But a planned neighbourhood needs some sort of authority overseeing its creation, which for Lawrence Park was the landowner, as it was for most early planned neighbourhoods. The Beaches had no such authority. Nobody was in charge. This absence of planning meant several things: no prescribed or prohibited types of housing, minimal public space, no neighbourhood community centre, little correspondence between street function and layout, and an ill-considered street grid in which streets might run headlong up the steepest grade, topography be damned, or dead-end at a property line. It also meant no attempt to create a community, or a neighbourhood in the social sense, as planners would strive to do a few decades later. Yet it also meant no controls or covenants barring residents on account of wealth, religion, or ethnicity; the neighbourhood was overwhelmingly Protestant Christian but that was a consequence of who chose to live in it, and of Toronto's demographic makeup, not of any policy or requirement.[54] The Beaches, for better or worse, was nobody's vision.

It was also entirely residential. Industry was nowhere to be found, and except for Queen Street, its main thoroughfare, commerce was absent as well. City directories and municipal assessment rolls show block after block, street after street, of residential buildings, with almost no sign of even a corner grocer or barber shop, let alone a factory or warehouse. Some tradesmen might have had backyard shops, but there is no record of this. The terms of Toronto's annexation prohibited "factories and hotels" in the Balmy Beach area as of 1909, a rather pointless prohibition with no record of being enforced; but even if it had been, it applied only to Balmy Beach, not to the neighbourhood overall.

The provincial Municipal Act of 1904 gave cities the power to enact zoning bylaws to exclude non-residential land uses from residential areas, but Toronto did not do so until 1912, by which time much of the Beaches was built.[55] So the only plausible explanation for this preponderance of residential buildings is that it made good business sense, that builders made more profit building houses than anything else. The residential character of the neighbourhood, like its range of house sizes, was created by the market, not by regulation.

As for the inhabitants of this streetcar suburb, occupational records suggest a wide range of what might be called, in the context of Edwardian urban society, the middle class.[56] The neighbourhood had numerous skilled tradesmen, in a great variety of trades, for whom working class might seem a more apt label, yet it also had plenty of clerical or administrative workers, sales personnel, and small business proprietors for whom that label does not quite fit, as well as the odd non-elite professional such as a pastor, accountant, or teacher. Top-level managers/proprietors and high-status professionals, and unskilled workers or labourers – which is to say the higher and lower classes – were present in much smaller numbers. So middle class, or perhaps more precisely lower middle class, seems correct. This is somewhat at odds with the standard interpretation, largely American, of streetcar suburbs as offering an escape from the city for the affluent middle class; this streetcar suburb might have offered an "escape" – although with no record of where residents previously lived, we know not what they were escaping – but for the financially secure working or lower middle class.[57]

Occupational records also reveal a degree of spatial differentiation by social status that matches that of the housing. The smaller houses on streets such as Waverley Road or Kenilworth Avenue in the west were likely to be home to bricklayers, teamsters, machinists, and carpenters, while the larger houses on Balsam Avenue or Spruce Hill Road in the east were likely to be home to merchants, managers, contractors, and the occasional barrister. But the caveat applied to the housing must be applied here as well – social diversity was the defining feature, not the spatial differentiation of that diversity. Assigning employed residents into two rather crude categories of high and low status, based entirely on occupation, of the ninety-seven residents of Waverley Road in 1910 just seventeen had high-status jobs whereas of the fifty-one residents of Balsam Road thirty-one had high-status jobs – a contrast, certainly, but these are the extremes.[58] Every one of the fully built-up streets sampled in this research had residents in both categories, and some had a nearly even split between the two.

Apart from the status of occupations, one is struck by the preponderance of private industry in the working lives of residents. Perhaps this should be expected of an urban neighbourhood built long before the explosion of public sector employment in the 1960s, but the numbers are striking nonetheless: of 433 employed pre-1914 residents counted in this study, the number of occupations dependent on the public purse – most of them professionals of not especially high status – can nearly be counted on one hand: a city fireman, an engineer with the provincial hydroelectric commission, another with the City Architect's Office, an architect with the Department of the Provincial Secretary, a school principal, and a librarian at the public library. Of course, the fact that residents' jobs were in private industry does not mean they were "industrial" jobs; service-sector jobs in printing, shipping, retailing, and insurance were common as well, at all status levels. The neighbourhood was, in short, part of an early industrial urban economy that included both service and manufacturing sectors.[59]

It is worth noting again how unprescribed all of this was. Affordable housing for people of modest income, a mix of social classes, minimal socio-economic spatial differentiation – these are objectives of modern-day city planning. Here they were achieved with no planning at all. Yet as critical as profit-seeking entrepreneurship was to the neighbourhood's physical and social genesis, it would be a mistake to see what emerged as entirely the product of free enterprise. This new streetcar suburb was unplanned, and its creation barely regulated, but it certainly did not lack public investment by an active and expanding municipal government.

CHAPTER FOUR

The Suburb and the City

Over the same years that Beaches' landowners, homebuilders, and residents were creating a suburban neighbourhood, the city of Toronto, like major cities the world over, was experiencing what can only be described as transformative growth. Numbers alone reveal the magnitude of the change.[1] Toronto's population rose, in round figures, from 86,000 in 1881 to 534,000 in 1914, the result of more residents within the city's original boundaries and the expansion of those boundaries to include newly built areas on the periphery. Measures of economic growth are equally striking: municipal property assessment rose from $53 million in 1881 to $309 million in 1911, and the annual value of building permits increased, in a much shorter time span, from $3.6 million in 1901 to $24.4 million in 1911. All of this is to say that in the space of two generations, Toronto evolved from a mid-sized commercial-industrial city into a metropolis – a regionally preponderant one too, as it rose from 4.5 per cent of Ontario's population in 1881 to 14.9 per cent in 1911.

Much of its new population came from abroad, for Toronto received a good share of Canada's immigrants in these years of famously heavy immigration – not all turn-of-the-century migrants were bound for prairie homesteads. In a way, this was nothing new. Toronto had always been a city of immigrants. In fact, the proportion of Toronto's population born outside Canada in 1911 (38 per cent) was slightly lower than it had been in 1881 (40 per cent) – reflecting a growing permanent population.[2] What distinguishes these years was a change, modest but significant, in the origin of its immigrants. For years Toronto's immigrants had come overwhelmingly from the British Isles, but an increasing number now came from elsewhere; from 1881 to 1911 the proportion of "foreign-born" in Toronto, defined in the census as neither British nor Canadian born, nearly doubled, from 5 per cent to 9 percent. The greatest number, by far, were Eastern European Jews, of which Toronto census takers counted only 124 in 1881 but 18,237 in 1911, an increase from 0.12 per cent to 4.8 per cent of the city's population. The city in 1911 was still 86.4 per cent "British" – an ethnic category that included Canadian – but it had taken its first step towards becoming a polyglot North American city.

Along with this expansion came more municipal administration. Part of this was just a response to the greater population – more property taxes to collect, more fires to put out – but not all. Toronto in these years, like most North American cities, went through what has long been called an age of reform, a roughly thirty-year period that saw governments, primarily municipal and provincial, introduce numerous programs meant to make life healthier, safer, and more humane.[3] Public health regulations and child welfare services are perhaps the best known. But municipal governments also created public parks and playgrounds, improved public water and sewer services, took over some private utilities, and introduced land use controls and building standards, and these actions were inspired by the reform spirit as well. Most reforms were enabled by provincial legislation, but new programs and facilities, once in place, were usually run and paid for by cities. Volunteer agencies, many of them run by religious bodies, provided valuable new services too, but cities carried much of the burden. This transformed municipal budgets. Expenditures by the Works Department, for example, rose from $596,000 in 1897 to $5.46 million in 1911.[4] Toronto's huge city hall, built in 1898, is not just a splendid work of municipal architecture; it is also a physical manifestation of increased municipal administration.

How did this affect a peripheral neighbourhood such as the Beaches? First, as noted earlier, when the residential neighbourhood began taking shape, in the 1890s, only its southwest quarter was within the city. Not until 1909 was the entire neighbourhood part of Toronto. This change came about through three separate annexations. In 1908 Toronto annexed the municipality of East Toronto, the southern portion of which was most of the Balmy Beach subdivision; then in 1909 it annexed the large unincorporated area north of Queen Street between Toronto and East Toronto (sometimes labelled Midway), which included the northwestern portion of the Beaches, and a few blocks of York Township east of Willow Avenue – the easternmost strip of the Balmy Beach subdivision (the portion in Lot 1) and the Monro estate property east of that, neither of which had been in East Toronto (figure 11).[5] Only then, strictly speaking, was the Beaches a Toronto neighbourhood.

Did this matter? In some ways, yes. Whether or not a property lay within the city of Toronto determined what municipal regulations applied and what services were available, as well as how much property tax its landowners paid. But in more fundamental ways the municipal boundary made little difference. Toronto's demographic and economic growth was a regional phenomenon, felt well beyond the city's boundary. This is unmistakable in the case of the Beaches, for it was the housing demand engendered by Toronto's business and employment growth that brought the residential neighbourhood into existence. Nearly all employed Beaches residents worked in Toronto,[6] and most of the land within the neighbourhood had been owned for years by people who lived in Toronto. So economically if not jurisdictionally the entire neighbourhood – not just the southwest corner of it – had been part of Toronto all along, and one suspects that most of its residents, and even most municipal administrators, saw it as part of the city long before it was annexed. All told, the fact that prior to 1908 three-quarters of the neighbourhood lay outside Toronto, though not irrelevant, is less important than one might think.

How was the Beaches affected by the social transformation brought on by the arrival of non-British immigrants? The impact of immigration on a single neighbourhood is hard to measure because the census districts used in the Canadian census in these years usually included multiple city neighbourhoods. We can assume that much of the Beaches' population came from abroad – some 38 per cent of Toronto's 1911 population was born outside Canada, and there is no reason to think the Beaches was much different.[7] And in fact data from the census district of Toronto East, which included the Beaches, lends support to this – nearly 37 per cent of the district's 1911 population was born outside Canada. But when one examines the *origins* of the foreign-born population, important differences appear: 85.9 per cent of Toronto East's foreign-born population was born in the British Isles, compared with 74.4 per cent for Toronto overall. Much more striking is that in the census district of Toronto Centre, where most recent immigrants were settling, just 47.3 per cent of the foreign-born population was born in the British Isles. Toronto Centre's population in 1911 was 19.5 per cent European-born; Toronto East's was 1.7 per cent. This pattern, one might note, had been set earlier – in 1901, when Toronto's eastern boundary was still at Greenwood Avenue, only five of Toronto's 3,034 Jews and only four of its 1,025 Italians resided east of Parliament Steet. Evidently, little of the city's new "foreign" element was settling east of the Don River, let alone as far east as the Beaches.[8] Unlike Toronto overall, the Beaches was not on its way to becoming a polyglot community.

***

The Beaches did, however, share in the benefits of Toronto's new and improved municipal services, one of the most visible of which was a major public park. Reformers within the Parks Department and on city council had wanted a park in the Beaches for several years. The City considered purchasing the sites of Victoria Park in 1904 and then Munro Park when it closed in 1906 – neither of which was within the city boundary, one might note. And it very nearly made a formal offer to buy the large old farm fronting the lake between Leuty and Maclean Avenues, owned and worked by the Sisters of Providence since 1896, before the Toronto Railway Company secured it for a new amusement park (see chapter 5). All these had been rejected by council.[9] Then in the fall of 1907 the parks commissioner informed council that his department had begun negotiating with the Williams family to purchase Kew Gardens for use as a public park. Council immediately endorsed the move and passed a bylaw to enable the purchase.[10]

It would not be a simple acquisition.[11] Kew Gardens itself was purchased easily enough, for $43,000, but the City did not consider this enough land for the park, so it sought surrounding property too. Williams and his family members owned some of it, but in separate lots, which required separate purchases. In addition, the family had already sold much of the eastern edge of their land, in individual lots fronting on Lee Avenue, and many of these lots now had houses on them; it had also leased thirteen lakefront lots on which lessees had built cottages. The family had even begun subdividing and selling building lots in the northwest corner of Kew Gardens (for none of these transactions had they registered plans of subdivision) and at least one of these buyers had begun building a house.[12] All these owners and lessees had to be bought out. When the process began, the assessment commissioner estimated an overall cost of $125,000 for what would be 20.19 acres of parkland, and nothing suggests he was far off the mark. Negotiations went on for several months and concluded in early 1908.[13]

We know little about what stood in Kew Gardens when the City acquired it. We do know that Williams lived in a house on the property because he is on record refusing to sell it. At first City negotiators agreed, but council ultimately decided otherwise and expropriated the house and the driveway to it from Lee Avenue (for $4,000). The deal permitted Mr. and Mrs. Williams to continue living there as renters (for $180 per annum), although if they did it was not for long because the house was gone by 1910.[14] Nearly everything else on the site was removed as well, including the lakefront cottages, which the City, having acquired them in its purchase, sold intact to buyers willing to move them off the property.[15] It left two cottages in place in the southeast part of the property. One was the large lakefront cottage owned by street railway executive James Gunn; he was also allowed to remain as a tenant (for $250 per season). The other was the unusual stone cottage Williams's son Kew had recently built for himself and his new wife on one of the Lee Avenue lots (which the City acquired from him for $4,750 "after lengthy negotiations").[16] The City also opted to retain Williams's name for the place – Kew Gardens – forever to confound visitors expecting something horticulturally notable in what is just a basic public park.

The City's commitment to enhancing its public realm did not go much beyond purchasing the land. Upholding its long-standing tradition of fiscal parsimony, council initially allotted just $3,000 for park improvements, effectively ruling out the sort of large-scale creative landscaping that other cities had done in their major public parks.[17] It filled the low, swampy ground towards the lake – the expense of which would boost adjacent property assessments, the assessment commissioner noted – but altered the overall grading very little and left most of the mature trees as they were. Photographs from five years after the City acquired the property show the northern portion with a swing set and some well-tended grass tennis courts, both of which the City likely had added, but the southern portion, which the City had filled, remained unlandscaped and still slightly rough.[18] By that time, however, the department had increased the park's capital budget enough to allow construction of a new building on the beach, from which the private cottages had been cleared – a one-storey, stone-walled bathing station ("change rooms" in modern parlance) with an open-air but fully covered rooftop sitting area (figure 14).

The City Engineer's Department, with responsibility for roads and bridges and all piped infrastructure, was at the forefront of the City's expansion of services.[19] Its work touched the Beaches in several ways, at least the part within Toronto, for in this case the municipal boundary did matter. It improved the surface of most public streets and built new sidewalks alongside them, and it played a part in facilitating the transition from private to public electricity supply (a separate municipal body, the Toronto Hydro Electric System, was formed to provide electricity in 1911).[20] But the undertaking that most affected the neighbourhood, and to

Figure 14. Kew Gardens shelter in 1913, soon after its completion. This view is looking south, from the park, showing the back of the structure. The building fronted on the lake, which is indiscernible in the hazy distance. The Lombardy poplars, partly obscured by the building, would have been planted when private cottages lined the beach of Joseph Williams's Kew Gardens.

City of Toronto Archives (Series 372, Sub-series 52, Item 218)

which the department probably made its greatest city-wide investment of money and effort, was the construction of water and sewer infrastructure.

Toronto had established a public waterworks several decades earlier, in 1874, and as the city grew the City Engineer's Department had extended its network of supply pipes as fast as staff and budgets permitted, adding five to ten miles of new watermains each year from 1895 to 1914.[21]

Watermains had not yet reached the Beaches when the first houses went in on Kippendavie and Kenilworth Avenues in the 1890s, so early residents there relied on community wells with hand-operated pumps, as cottagers had for some time. By 1900 watermains had arrived, under Queen Street, and the City began running supply pipes beneath the residential streets as demand warranted. Waverley Road south of Queen Street was the first served, in 1900 – the subdivider of this property seems to have been particularly adept at getting houses built on his lots – and other streets soon followed.[22] By 1905 the entire southwest corner of the Beaches, the portion within Toronto, had piped water available to any property owners who wanted to connect to and pay for the service.

The Balmy Beach area, being outside Toronto, had no city water. In 1904 the municipality of East Toronto built a small waterworks beside the Balmy Beach clubhouse that drew in, filtered, and pumped lake water up to a standpipe (an inexpensive type of columnar water tower) at the southeast corner of Gerrard and Wayland, and it began offering gravity-pressure water service, street by street, to those who wanted to pay for it.[23] We know this waterworks was built because one of the terms of annexation was that Toronto assume the debt East Toronto had incurred to build it. And Toronto's City Engineer's Department, upon taking over the system, reported some 50,000 feet of existing watermains.[24] But we have no indication how many residents purchased the service. Memoirs of the early days in Balmy Beach mention street-corner water pumps, which drew up groundwater, but say nothing about piped-in water, so we might assume this rather primitive waterworks was not very effective, or popular.[25]

Sewer service was not provided anywhere in the Beaches until early 1907 when the City built a basic sewage treatment plant – essentially large above-ground sedimentation and filtration tanks – at Woodbine Beach and laid sewage collection pipes under the nearby streets, all of which, again, were within city jurisdiction (figure 15).[26] Piped-in water supply, of course, makes piped-out sewage disposal nearly essential, so this sequence of events is understandable. Prior to this, residents would have had backyard privies. Balmy Beach in 1906 had no sewers and no plan to get them, so its residents also relied on privies – for which the sandy soil was ideal, a reporter explained.[27] The municipality of East Toronto never built sewers in Balmy Beach.

Nearly everything relating to piped services changed after 1910. The City Engineer's Department began raising the standard of service in annexed areas by improving their existing infrastructure and/or extending the City's systems into them.[28] The City by then had also begun upgrading its own services: it built a larger-capacity and higher-pressure water supply, and, after years of delay, committed to build a city-wide interceptor sewer that would "intercept" downward flowing sewers before they reached the lake and carry their contents to a new central treatment plant at Ashbridge's Bay.[29] The new interceptor ran under Kingston Road in the east end. The City also built a smaller interceptor sewer under the full length of Queen Street to convey sewage from residential areas north of the street (all at a higher elevation than the street) directly to the new treatment plant, not

Figure 15. Woodbine Sewage Disposal Works, c. 1907. This ultimately short-lived facility, situated on what is now Woodbine Beach Park, served from about 1907 to 1914. This view, looking southwest, shows the old Woodbine Beach curving into the distance (upper centre, with trees), and behind it (upper right) Ashbridge's Bay and marsh in their natural state.

City of Toronto Archives (Series 376, File 5, Item 74)

utilizing the main interceptor under Kingston Road.[30] This was followed, a few years later, by a new interceptor sewer along the lakefront that collected sewage from the residential streets below Queen and conveyed it west as far as a new pumping station at Woodbine Avenue – replacing the now inadequate Woodbine disposal works – which pumped sewage up to the main interceptor a few hundred metres north.[31]

By 1914 the City Engineer's Department had furnished the neighbourhood with a reliable, well-pressurized supply of clean water and a sewer system that conveyed all locally produced sewage hundreds of metres west, away from the neighbourhood's groundwater and beaches. The City had built and paid for all this. It is worth noting, though, that a good part of what the City spent had come from the neighbourhood's property owners, and not just through their property taxes: Any landowner in Toronto who dIrectly benefited from a public work was subject to a "local improvement charge" set by the City Engineer. Charges of this sort, with various names, have a long history in municipal administration, and the City of Toronto made good use of them in these reform years. They did not cover the entire cost of improvements – property tax revenue covered the greatest share – but they made a contribution. In 1908, for example, the City Engineer reported city-wide expenditures of $3.074 million on public works and revenue of $1.3 million from local improvement charges.[32]

***

These reform years also saw Toronto introduce its first land-use zoning. The principle of zoning was, and still is, that the state, acting in the broad public interest, has a right to regulate what private owners can and cannot build, and do, on their land in certain areas, or zones. The idea emerged in late-nineteenth-century Germany, mostly for extensions to existing cities, where such restrictions were deemed necessary to ensure that newly urbanized areas functioned properly.[33] It infringed on property owners' freedom to do as they wished with their property, of course, and German landowners resisted at first, but it took root nonetheless, partly because a social reform spirit was alive in Germany at the time but also because landowners recognized that such restrictions could enhance land values and thus be to their advantage. The idea soon found its way to

North America, where for various reasons it was used more to protect existing areas from change than to prescribe the form of new urban areas, its original purpose.

Zoning first appeared in Ontario in a 1904 amendment to the Municipal Act that gave cities the power to prohibit non-residential land uses that were deemed noxious – such as commercial laundries, slaughterhouses, and factories – in certain locations.[34] This is what empowered Toronto, in 1908, to prohibit factories in the Balmy Beach subdivision. The legislation's scope was expanded in 1912 by an amendment that permitted cities to prohibit apartment buildings in residential neighbourhoods.[35] This move to classify apartment buildings as, essentially, a noxious activity was made largely at the behest of Toronto city council. Toronto was being swamped with apartment buildings in these years, or so many residents believed; city council requested the power to control their construction and the Province of Ontario responded with this amendment. Once empowered, council promptly enacted a bylaw prohibiting them on nearly every residential street in the city.[36] This antipathy towards apartment buildings, insofar as it can be explained at all, seems to have been based on a presumed association of apartments with libertine lifestyles and with poverty and crime and, of course, with correspondingly lower property values. Whether or not these concerns were well-founded, or the actions they prompted sensible, Toronto's Edwardian apartment phobia yielded a bylaw that shaped the city's physical form for years to come.

But none of these restrictions had much impact on the Beaches. By the time the apartment prohibition was applied, no earlier than 1913, much of the neighbourhood was already built. It had few apartment buildings, but this was simply because builders had not built them. The bylaw would have some impact later, in the building boom of the 1920s, though even then its prohibition was not as strictly applied as is sometimes supposed (chapter 5). The earlier provincial legislation, empowering cities to prohibit noxious industries and commerce, also appears to have had no impact, for there is no sign of any such restrictions being enacted, other than for Balmy Beach – where they seem never to have been used. The absence of industry is better explained by the absence of railway lines, and this resulted from decisions made decades earlier by railway companies, while the absence of commerce on residential streets, like the absence of apartment buildings, seems to have resulted from local builders, through their own volition, choosing not to build commercial buildings anywhere other than the main street. If conflicts arose over the use of land for industrial or commercial purposes, they must have been minor or short-lived because none appear in official records. There is, all told, no sign of Toronto's zoning bylaws having much impact on the formation of the neighbourhood.

***

A related municipal reform – the introduction of building regulations or building controls – might have had some impact. Like most cities Toronto already had a long history of stipulating where, how, and with what materials buildings could be built, the main objective being to minimize the risk of fire.[37] In fact the city's very first bylaw, enacted upon municipal incorporation in 1834, was to limit the use of inflammable building materials, especially wood, and this bylaw was followed by others. How rigorously these were enforced has never been closely studied, although the fact that they were revised over the decades makes one think that builders had to respect them. The 1874 bylaw, which regulated, in its words, "the erection of buildings and the storage of inflammable materials," looks to have been the first to introduce the concept of "Fire Limits" – precisely defined districts in which certain building materials must or must not be used, essentially a very specific sort of zoning.[38] It set out three such Limits ranging from Limit A for the dense old city where buildings had to be of brick or stone to Limit C, further out, where wooden structures were permitted under certain conditions. An 1890 bylaw redrew some of the Limit boundaries and added a fourth. A 1904 bylaw went further, and a 1913 bylaw further still.[39]

Fire Limits arrived in the southwest part of the Beaches with the 1890 bylaw, which extended Limit D out to the eastern city boundary. Within this Limit wooden structures were permitted only if they were roofed with incombustible material.[40] The 1904 bylaw retained the same restrictions (relabelling it Fire Limit C) but sharpened the language, and required that *all* exterior materials on wooden frame buildings, not just the roof, be incombustible: "… the wood work forming the outside walls shall be either veneered with brick or other non-combustible material, or be lathed, plastered and roughcast, or stuccoed."[41] One might then assume that any house built in this part of the Beaches after 1890 would have an incombustible roof, and if built after 1904 would be clad entirely in either brick or plaster. But one would be mistaken. Many of the houses built along Kippendavie,

Kenilworth, and Waverley in the 1890s, while the 1890 bylaw was in effect, were framed and clad in wood.[42] Indeed, one of the most celebrated buildings in the area, the house that architect Charles F. Wagner designed and had built for himself in 1901 on Waverley Road, called Inglenook, was one such house. As was another of Wagner's design built the following year across the street from his own (figure 16; see also figure 13).[43] Whether these early houses were roofed as the bylaw required is hard to say; documentary sources do not reveal such details, and most houses built at this early stage have been demolished or substantially rebuilt and their original roofs are long gone. But one suspects they were not. Wagner's two houses, which were photographed soon after their construction, certainly look to be roofed with wood shingles. Some lesser quality houses were photographed prior to their demolition around 1930, and although the photographs do not clearly show roof materials the houses do not look as if they met building bylaws of any sort. Some are little more than shacks.[44]

Moreover, we know that builders continued building wooden-clad houses on these streets after 1904, apparently in contravention of the new, stricter bylaw. Many houses still stand with their wood cladding in full view. A close reading of the bylaw, however, explains this irregularity. In addition to extending the incombustible requirement to all exterior walls, the bylaw added a clause – now easily overlooked – stating that the requirement did not apply to structures under thirty-five feet in height, which all residential buildings in the area were.[45] It offers no explanation for this backtracking. But the housing historian Richard Harris, in his study of these

Figure 16. A lesser-known work of architect C.F. Wagner's, this south-facing, wooden-clad house on the west side of Waverley Road, built in 1902 for local businessman George A. White, is shown here soon after its 1907 purchase by the noted oologist Walter Raine, who had evidently put a substantial addition on the front to accommodate his family. It was demolished in the 1960s. This photograph, held by Raine's descendants, appeared in an article on him in the ornithology periodical *Blue Jay* 39, no. 3 (September 1981).

Courtesy of *Blue Jay* Magazine and Nature Saskatchewan

regulations, unwittingly offers one with his finding that some builders opposed the City's brick requirement, saying that it raised the cost of their houses.[46] No doubt it did. And considering what has been observed in the previous chapter about the importance of small, low-priced houses in the early housing market, the builders' opposition is understandable. Perhaps their protestations, along with an apparent disregard of the earlier bylaw, prompted the City to loosen the regulation for this peripheral Fire Limit in the 1904 bylaw. Whatever the cause, this explicit exemption, together with the extensive earlier use of wood, suggests that even in the part of the neighbourhood under City jurisdiction the 1904 bylaw had minimal impact on the exterior of Beaches housing.

Confounding this irregularity, however, is the fact that brick construction became increasingly common after 1904 nearly everywhere in the neighbourhood.[47] Maybe it was not required, but it was done. Brick is especially noticeable in the centre of the neighbourhood, where on three new streets laid out in a 1905 plan of subdivision for land north of Queen Street – Lee (east side), Hambly (both sides), and Wineva (west side) – all but 16 of the 164 houses built on those streets by 1913 were brick.[48] Noteworthy, however, is that most of this property, while outside the city boundary when subdivided, was built up after it became part of the city in the Midway annexation of 1909. Evidently, either the sellers of the lots or the builders who bought them waited until the land was in Toronto before proceeding with development. But why would builders wait until a brick bylaw applied – especially one they could avoid – before building brick houses?[49] One plausible explanation is that builders were waiting for their lots to have Toronto water and sewer services, or at least be on the verge of having them, for if one intends to build and sell better-quality, higher-priced brick houses – believing there is good profit in doing so – one needs fully serviced lots to build them on. Who would buy a premium-priced house that required a back-yard privy when houses a few blocks away had piped water and sewer service? Perhaps it was not building bylaws but piped services that brought brick construction to the Beaches.[50]

Inflammability of a structure's exterior was not the only concern of the bylaws. Structural stability was important too. In fact, the 1913 bylaw has as much to say about structure as fire retardance. Large and/or tall public buildings, particularly theatres, were the bylaw's prime focus, but it applied to residential buildings too, and for them the most strictly prescribed structural element was the foundation. Foundations were especially important for houses with brick exteriors, which are much heavier than wood exteriors. The 1890 bylaw prohibited construction of any brick or brick-veneered building on a wooden foundation (it placed no restrictions on the foundations of wooden buildings).[51] But the thickness of the foundation, not just its material, was critical too, and for this the 1904 bylaw introduced specific requirements: foundation walls for structures with brick exteriors had to be fourteen inches thick if of brick and sixteen inches thick if of stone, while those with wood or stucco exteriors had to be at least nine inches thick and of brick.[52] Both the 1904 and the 1913 bylaws set out specifications for concrete foundations as well, an increasingly popular but not yet fully understood structural material (figure 17).

A finished building's foundation is not as easy to see as its exterior cladding so without intrusive basement investigations one cannot determine whether these structural requirements were followed in houses that still stand. Signs

Figure 17. The concrete foundation has failed in this pair of brick-walled, semi-detached houses, 67 and 69 Kippendavie, in 1913. It is one of three such structures – six homes – a builder was squeezing onto a single large lot, the first brick structures on the street. The foundation of his adjacent structure, 63/65 Kippendavie, also failed. The City Architect's Department inspected, and photographed, the failures.

City of Toronto Archives (Series 372, Sub-series 1, Item 20)

are that they were. Houses erected after about 1910 seem better built, or at least they remain sufficiently square and stable to be either still standing or to have attracted major renovations. But, again, it is hard to attribute this entirely to the building bylaw. Houses were built on solid foundations in Balmy Beach before annexation imposed the Toronto bylaw.[53] And since any competent builders knew that brick houses needed robust foundations – we should not forget that these bylaws were nothing more than a codification of what skilled tradesmen already knew – better foundations may simply be a consequence of more brick construction rather than the bylaw per se.

One begins to suspect that, while the building bylaws cannot be entirely discounted, what one is seeing here is builders responding to an increasingly affluent market. Builders knew that good quality housing, with solid foundations and well-laid structural brick walls, cost more to build than poorer quality housing, and likely would have built it only when confident of recovering their greater costs in the sale of what they built – which by 1910 most apparently believed they could do. The problem is that affluent buyers and city bylaws appeared at around the same time and disentangling one from the other is next to impossible. One can probably say that by 1910 Toronto building bylaws were having at least some impact on the physical form of the neighbourhood, but they were by no means the only, or even the prime, factor at work. This leads to the intriguing conclusion that the City produced sounder, better-quality housing in the Beaches not by legally requiring it but by introducing the water and sewer services, public parks, and public schools that made the neighbourhood attractive to those who could afford to buy sounder, better-quality housing.

***

There is no escaping the fact that Toronto played a central role in creating the Beaches, as both a (lower case) city – a concatenation of people and human endeavour – and a (upper case) City – a corporate entity that passed bylaws and raised and spent public funds. The former's growing population and expanding economy sparked the neighbourhood's genesis; the latter's investment into urban infrastructure and public space, as well as, to a degree, its regulation of the urbanization process, enhanced its livability. Or one might say, in slightly different terms, that the Beaches was a product of both private and public initiative, of both the commercial and the guardian syndromes, to employ Jane Jacobs's insightful but often overlooked dichotomy.[54] Private landowners in search of profit carved out and sold lots to speculators and builders, who in turn built houses in a style and spatial arrangement that maximized their profit. A private street railway carried residents to and from the neighbourhood, charging fares high enough to pay its employees and yield profit for its owners. Profit-seeking entrepreneurs risked capital by establishing shops and services along main street. A large private (soon to be public) electricity provider and a large private (never to be public) telephone company put up poles and wires to convey and sell their products and services to residents, for a profit. But alongside all this private enterprise the City, using revenue raised through the property tax and local improvement charges, paved streets and sidewalks, laid water and sewer pipes, and created public parks; school boards, with funds also procured entirely from the property tax, built and operated schools, while Christian congregations – non-profit bodies using funds privately raised among their members – built churches. These actions were critical as well, for without

Figure 18. Queen Street, 1904, looking northwest from the south side, just west of Lee Avenue, the unbuilt land that would become Bellefair and Wheeler Avenues in the distance. This single photograph depicts many elements of the emerging streetcar suburb: watermains, streetcar tracks (and waiting passengers), shops with consumer goods (being delivered by horse and sleigh?), and maybe most telling of all is that much that is seen in the picture, the commercial building and the land beside it, is for sale.

City of Toronto Archives (Series 376, File 4, Item 35)

them the profit seekers could not and would not have done what they did. Largely uncoordinated and entirely unplanned, this hybrid process somehow produced a functional, socially balanced suburban residential neighbourhood (figure 18).

CHAPTER FIVE

Filling the Gaps

By 1914 the neighbourhood's basic physical form had been set. Most of its residential streets had been laid out and built up, several major public buildings had been erected, and the essential physical infrastructure was in place. Two large tracts of land, however, remained undeveloped. One was the land either side of a deep, wooded ravine running north to south through the central part of the neighbourhood; the other was the site of an extensive amusement park that the Toronto Railway Company had opened in 1907 south of Queen Street, slightly west of the ravine. Both would become residential districts in the 1920s.

They would be built up in a manner quite different from that of the earlier subdivisions, reflecting a new residential development process that was emerging in the 1920s. Both were much larger than the pre-1914 subdivisions, and both were owned and actively developed by a corporate entity, closely related corporate entities as it happened; gone were the days of private landowners subdividing and building up individual blocks of land.

Both were planned to a degree as well. Urban planning had come a long way, internationally at least, from its birth some twenty years earlier, and by the 1920s it was being pursued in and around major cities in several parts of the world, at both a city-wide and a neighbourhood scale. In Toronto, however, it had not come far. Toronto had a City Surveyor (monitoring lot layouts) and a City Architect (regulating building structure) but no planning department, and it showed no sign of wanting one, with many city councillors seeming to believe it would be imprudent, bordering on irresponsible, to allow unelected professionals, whether city staff or contracted consultants, to determine the city's form and function.[1] The city did have a few practising landscape designers and town planners, and they were available for any person or institution wanting to engage them, but work was scarce. Planning was possible in Toronto in the interwar years, but it was by no means established or required.[2] Reflecting this, one of these interwar developments was fully planned by its corporate owner – in the sense of it being a single, coordinated undertaking, laid out and designed according to a particular vision – while the other was planned only in the most basic sense of the word. The residential enclaves produced on these two tracts thus stand out not only from the pre-1914 built landscape around them but also from each other.

As for broader oversight of the development process, the situation was essentially what it had been before the war –

provincial law still required subdividers to register plans of subdivision, but not much more than that. The City and Suburbs Act of 1912 had strengthened provincial control somewhat, stipulating that a plan's lots and streets had to "conform as far as practicable with any plan so adopted or approved" before it could be registered.[3] But this was having minimal impact in Toronto because the City had no "adopted or approved" plan to which individual plans had to conform. The City still monitored street widths, lot lines, and now more than ever the stability of structures, and it had enacted some neighbourhood-specific zoning bylaws – all of which are noted above – but it used its powers prudently. Most streets, houses, and open spaces still went where the property owners developing the land wanted them to go.

***

The lands in and alongside the ravine were part of Lot 3, First Concession, of the original colonial survey. The entire lot had been initially granted, in 1797, to Jean-Baptiste Bouchette, a naval officer and one-time political client of Lord Dorchester, and over the following fifty-some years it passed through the hands of several members of the colonial elite, among them the quintessential Family Compact placeman Darcy Boulton (1759–1834) and his extended family, and as it did it was broken into smaller parcels, each with a different owner. The ravine portion south of Kingston Road was one of those parcels, and in 1856 it was obtained by the well-connected, English-born barrister Alexander Leith.[4] There is no sign of Leith or the earlier owners clearing or making use of this land, probably because its hills and soggy bottomlands were ill-suited to farming, so it remained in its natural state. But by the 1870s, with the pioneer era giving way to the urban era throughout the district, this tract of unspoiled forest and streams had begun acquiring new value – looking less like unusable land and more like a potential suburban estate, at least to those of sufficient means. And in 1872 it was purchased for this very purpose by the local clergyman William Stewart Darling.[5]

Darling is usually identified as the rector of an Anglican parish in Scarborough Township, which he was, but either he or his wife had family money because he not only purchased the property but also built a substantial home at its north end, on high ground overlooking the ravine, not something one did on a rural pastor's stipend.[6] It was Darling who bestowed the name Glen Stewart on the property, Stewart being his own middle (and thus perhaps his mother's family) name. We know little about Darling's house or what use he made of it. He advertised it for rent to a "yearly tenant" in 1881, so he was clearly not living in it, at that time at least.[7] Darling died in 1886 and the property fell to his son Frank (b. 1850), soon to be an accomplished Toronto architect, who rented the house to various wealthy Torontonians for several years.[8] The upper-class cottage scene was developing along the lake by then, and the area had acquired some cachet. In the fall of 1900, Frank Darling sold the entire property to one of those wealthy Torontonians, Alfred Ernest Ames, a financier who dwelt at the highest level of wealth and status in Toronto's business world. Ames's attainment of such heights had been helped by his marriage to Mary Cox, daughter of George Albertus Cox, an even wealthier financier of the previous generation who held controlling interest in several major Toronto financial institutions. Cox, a Liberal supporter, had been appointed to the Senate by Wilfrid Laurier in 1896.[9]

Ames renovated and expanded the house and set about acquiring adjacent properties, eventually owning everything fronting the south side of Kingston Road between Lee and Beech Avenues, and most of the ravine and the sloping land either side of it down to Queen Street (except for the substantial Howard property on the lower east edge of the ravine). He had his groundskeepers cut carriage roads and pathways through the woods, impound the spring-fed stream to create ponds stocked with trout, and even landscape a small golf course on the northwestern portion.[10] Ames invested heavily into the property, making it, a newspaper report declared, "one of the finest suburban homes in Ontario" (figure 19).[11] But clearly he had overextended himself, and his business, for in June 1903 A.E. Ames & Co. suddenly suspended financial transactions and effectively shut down. It soon became known that the company's stock holdings had lost so much value in a business downturn that they no longer sufficed as security for its substantial debts, leaving Ames teetering on personal bankruptcy. He was saved from this embarrassment by his father-in-law, G.A. Cox, who bought the entire hundred-acre estate as well as Ames's family home on Sherbourne Street, giving Ames enough cash to weather the storm.[12]

Relations between the two men, financial and personal, are hard to discern. One of the two, presumably Cox, seems to have tried to sell the entire property to the City in 1904 for

Figure 19. The south-facing front of the Glen Stewart manor house, as it looked in 1905.

Toronto Daily Star, 10 May 1905, p. 5; courtesy of Toronto Public Library, Special Collections

use as a park (the City was seeking parkland at the time).[13] It is hard to imagine Ames favouring this course of action, so there may have been some tension. Yet there must also have been some goodwill, for Ames and his family remained in their Sherbourne Street house with Cox, who lived next door, as its owner.[14] The Glen Stewart property looks to have remained mostly in Cox's hands too. In the summer of 1905, and perhaps 1906, the house was "placed at the disposal" of the Governor General and his entourage for a week to allow the vice-regal party to prepare for and attend the King's Plate horse race at nearby Woodbine Park.[15]

Surely this was arranged by Senator Cox. A newspaper article about the rental does identify the house as Ames's summer residence, but this probably reflects how the place was viewed, not who owned it. In 1909 Ames and his family vacated their Sherbourne Street house and took up full-time residence at Glen Stewart, which would have solidified that public perception.[16]

The most definitive evidence of Cox's ownership comes from a series of property transactions in 1909, perhaps done in conjunction with Ames's move, which laid the foundation for the property's transformation.[17] Records reveal that Cox transferred ownership of most of the western portion – including the house and the land around it – to National Trust (a Cox-controlled company). This land was heavily encumbered with mortgages, most of them held by Provident Investments (another Cox-controlled company). On the same day, he transferred the entire eastern portion, apparently free of mortgages, to Toronto Savings and Loan (another of his firms). Ames is not mentioned in these transactions. About a year later Toronto Savings and Loan acquired a few adjacent properties, some of which Ames had previously owned, and together with National Trust registered a preliminary plan of subdivision for the entire area.[18] Development did not ensue, for reasons not on record, and in the summer of 1912 Cox abruptly shifted course and again offered to sell it all to the City for a park, for $600,000. This elicited great excitement at city hall, where officials had coveted the fine, wooded property for some time. Strong opinions emerged both for and against the purchase – the price was no bargain, and development of Kew Gardens, which had cost one-fifth of that, was underway – but before council could make a final decision Cox, as unexpectedly as he had offered to sell, withdrew his offer and returned to his earlier plan.[19] He would do what the previous generation of landowners had done with such success – subdivide and sell the land for residential development (figure 20).

Ames, it should be noted, played almost no part in this. He emerged owning the western portion of his former estate with the house – the heavily mortgaged property Cox had transferred to National Trust. How Cox arranged this, and with what sentiments, we will never know. He may have had this outcome in mind from the start, wanting to ensure that his daughter and son-in-law were well housed while keeping the latter burdened with some consequences of his earlier profligacy.[20] Ames had no intention of selling the heavily mortgaged portion he now owned, understandable since he and his family had just settled into the house; newspaper coverage of the park purchase debate makes this clear, reporting that the City was considering just the eighty acres owned by Cox, not the twenty acres owned by Ames.[21] In the end, of course, Cox's land did not become a park, but the 80/20 split endured: only Cox's portion was given over to residential development, not Ames's.

Ames came through it all rather well. Cox died in 1914 leaving his daughter Mary "amply provided for" with property and stocks – surely helping Ames reduce whatever debts he was still carrying – and during the First World War he brought his financial firm back to profitability.[22] Always a public-spirited businessman, Ames became a noted philanthropist in the 1920s. He was especially generous to his

Figure 20. An unhurried stroll along a rustically fenced carriageway in Stewart Manor on what looks to be a special dress-up day. The archival record dates this photograph c. 1910, which, if true, means that much of the natural woodland they were enjoying would soon be given over to residential development.

City of Toronto Archives (Fonds 1244, Item 7231)

church, Beech Avenue Methodist, and as a supporter of Church Union he aided in its rebuilding as the new, larger Kingston Road United. He also opened his private golf course – which in 1922 lost six holes that had been on Cox-owned land then being developed – to public membership, creating what *Canadian Golfer* declared Ontario's first public course.[23] Ames died a respected man of affairs in 1934, leaving the aging manor house to his wife – his unmarried daughter and son had predeceased him – and, eventually, his name on a local street and public school.[24]

Cox's first step in developing the property was to transfer ownership of a large central portion of it from Toronto Savings and Loan to the Provident Investment Company, another of his financial enterprises.[25] Why he did this, and what benefit it yielded, is not apparent. But Provident was by then in the hands of his nephew Alfred Herbert Cox, and since the elder Cox was known, and in fact criticized, in these years for drifting into excessive nepotism, there may be no need for further explanation.[26] Cox had founded Provident in 1893, in Peterborough, as the Provident Investment and Mortgage Guarantee Corporation, and in 1899 he moved it to Toronto, shortened its name, and began investing its capital in property development.[27] His nephew entered the firm in 1906 and moved it further in that direction. The elder Cox must have thought the young man capable and experienced enough to orchestrate a large, complex, multi-year development project, and he seems to have been correct.

Provident then did what no other subdivider in the area had done: it engaged accomplished landscape architects to design its development, entrusting the job to the Toronto firm Dunington-Grubb & Harries. Howard Grubb and Lorrie Dunington were a pair of eccentric but talented English-born landscape designers who, combining their surnames upon marriage, had come to Toronto in 1911, established an office, and begun practising as professional partners in and around the city. They would continue to practise for decades, leaving a considerable mark on the regional landscape.[28] A year after opening their Toronto office they entered what turned out to be a short-lived partnership with American landscape designer W.E. Harries, whom they had met while studying at Cornell University. The project's design was clearly that partnership's work – the name Dunington-Grubb & Harries is on an extant blueprint of the plan – and must therefore have been completed sometime in 1913.[29]

Which of the three partners led the design is not known, but collectively the firm, working sensitively with the complex terrain, prepared a plan that laid out 170 building lots on streets curving along and down the ravine borders (figure 21). Their design could not serve as a registered plan, since the partners were not certified surveyors, so Provident engaged the experienced surveyors Speight & Van Nostrand to conduct a precise survey and, following the overall Dunington-Grubb & Harries scheme, to draw up a plan for the southern half of the property, which became the plan of record for this portion of the project.[30] At about this time – the precise chronology is hard to determine – Toronto Savings and Loan sold the southwest corner of its holding – what is now Hammersmith and Glen Manor, north of Islesworth – to the construction company Cox and Cummings, a firm co-owned by another of Cox's nephews (a brother of Alfred

Herbert), Frank Wallace Cox.[31] This sale, and the construction company's obvious intention to build on land it had just bought, brought the project's overall plan to the attention of the City Engineer, his concern being the intention to run roads along the sides of the ravine. The Engineer approved the design on the condition that the builders ensure their supporting earthworks and retaining walls were sufficient to render the roads "suitable for vehicular traffic."[32] The builders met this condition, for those roads – charming if perhaps overly narrow in places – have been bearing the weight of motor vehicles for over a century.

The development was conceived from the start as an upper-middle-class residential enclave, targeted at the suit-and-tie-wearing professional man and his family, making it comparable in some ways to Judge Wilson's initial vision for his Balmy Beach subdivision. But it differed in fundamental ways. It was to be truly designed, for one thing, which Balmy Beach was not. It was to consist of year-round suburban homes rather than summer residences, its lots were far smaller and its housing would be correspondingly more compact, and it made use of the rolling wooded terrain not the lake. It was also more likely to be a commercial success in the affluent 1920s than Wilson's undertaking had been in the 1870s. Provident began selling lots in early 1914, and some houses went up that year, but the war slowed progress and only after 1918 did lot sales, and house-building, pick up. The southern half, the area covered by the 1913 plan of subdivision, was developed first, through the early 1920s. The northern part did not see any housing until 1924.[33] The subdivision was not fully built up until the early 1930s, almost twenty years after lot sales began.

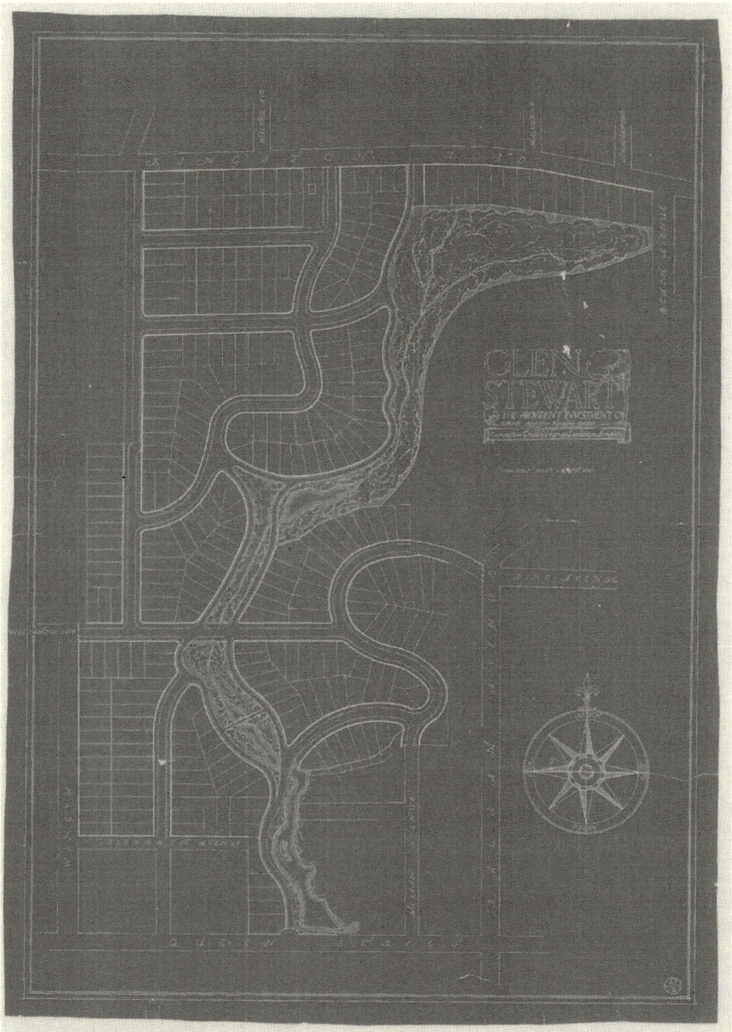

Figure 21. Dunington-Grubb & Harries, Landscape Architects, "Glen Stewart, The Provident Investment Company, Toronto" – a blueprint of the firm's design for Stewart Manor preserved in the papers of, and thus presumably at some point submitted to, the City Parks Department.

City of Toronto Archives (Series 724, Item 11)

Unlike the neighbourhood's prewar subdivisions, Stewart Manor, as it was formally named – no sign of "Ames" – was indeed somebody's vision. By no means were builders free to construct simply what they thought would sell. They could build only detached residential buildings with external walls of brick, stone, or cement; their buildings had to be designed by a certified architect, have a value of at least $5,000 on the ravine-facing streets ($3,500 elsewhere), and they could erect only one building on each thirty-foot lot (no further subdivision); no sand or earth could be removed from the lot (no alteration of the grades); and buildings, including front verandahs, could be no less than twenty feet from the street.[34] Provident's sales agents played up these restrictions in the advertising – claiming that they would protect your investment by ensuring that all residents were "the kind of people you would choose for neighbors."[35] The overall ambience was somewhat prescribed as well. Front fences could also be no less than twenty feet from the street unless they were "of open construction and not higher than three feet," and all fences were subject to Provident's approval; billboards and any other sort of advertising were prohibited, utility poles had to be placed behind the houses, and no existing trees could be cut down during construction. The upshot was a compact residential enclave of good-quality homes, many of them designed with nostalgic Tudor-revival details – the choice of owners and/or their architects, not a requirement of Provident – on lots with plenty of mature trees. The enclave remains to this day a distinctive, and by some measures the most attractive, part of the neighbourhood.[36] Here was the new development process: owned and initiated by a corporate owner, conceived as a coherent whole, designed by professionals, and sold in an affluent mass market.

The subdivision's design had left the stream bed, some swampy lands alongside it, and the steeper hillsides all in their natural state, and in 1931 as house-building neared completion Provident donated these lands, some eleven acres in all, to the City for use as a public park.[37] These lands were, of course, undevelopable and thus of little commercial value, and Provident's generosity should be viewed with this in mind, but it was a public-spirited gesture nonetheless, and the company did agree to throw in a few saleable residential lots to allow public access from street level down into the ravine. Before accepting the donation, however, the City insisted that Provident pay the more than $14,000 of local improvement charges accrued since 1928 for the sidewalks, sewer connections, and other "improvements" the City had built. Evidently the company did not object, for the matter disappears from the historical record, and the ravine lands, with several access paths and stairways, were soon placed under the jurisdiction of the Parks Department and given the official name Glen Stewart Park.

***

The amusement park property was Lot 3 of the "Broken Front" concession, below Queen Street. It too had been granted in 1797 and had passed through several elite speculator/owners – most of them the same as the ravine property owners – before being acquired in 1854 by the enterprising Scottish immigrant William R. Grahame.[38] It was likely an investment property for him too, for he is known to have owned and worked 1,200 acres in Vaughan Township where he built and operated a mill on the upper Humber River.[39] But in 1857, prior to returning to Scotland, Grahame sold the western half to a man named William Whittet, about whom nothing is known other than his being identified in the land transaction record as a "gardener" – the first indication that, unlike so much of the lower plain, the western part of this land was cultivable, and likely had been for some time, perhaps explaining Grahame's purchase. After several other transactions – one to another "market gardener" – the lot was acquired in its entirely by the prosperous King Street liquor merchant Thomas O'Connor, the eastern half in 1874 and the more valuable western half, encumbered by mortgages, not fully until 1880. O'Connor is on record as residing on the property in 1880 although, if he did, he would have had to travel to his King Street shop by private horse and carriage until horse-drawn streetcar service began in 1887.[40] Perhaps he resided mostly at his shop.

With O'Connor as its owner, it became known locally as "Thomas O'Connor's Farm," so it must still have been under cultivation.[41] It begins appearing in Toronto assessment rolls in the 1880s (it was within city limits), and these records list multiple buildings on the premises, one of them a substantial brick structure, maybe an old farmhouse.[42] They also reveal that O'Connor operated a hotel there for several years – a suitable enterprise for a liquor merchant with a large semi-rural property – presumably in the large brick building. Records also show at least one farmer (sometimes identified as a market gardener) living on the property, so parts were still being farmed. Other tenants are on record too, at various times.[43] The property remained in this state into the 1890s: a large, square block of land with a single owner, about forty acres in all, still essentially rural, with farm fields on its western half and a stream and extensive wetland on its eastern half, situated between the Balmy Beach subdivision to the east and Walter S. Lee's holdings to the west. The owners of those two properties were subdividing and selling in the 1890s. Thomas O'Connor was doing neither.

O'Connor died in 1895. Little is known about him, but he was apparently a devout Roman Catholic, or at least a staunch supporter of Catholic social action, for he bequeathed the entire property to the Sisters of St. Joseph, a centuries-old French religious order that had been providing education and social services in Toronto since the 1850s.[44] It is an intriguing bequest for a wealthy liquor merchant, and one suspects there is an equally intriguing story behind it that will remain forever untold. The Sisters took over the property and named it the House of Providence Farm, applying the name they had long used for their downtown house of refuge. They worked it, producing food for the indigent residents of their House, until 1906, when they sold it for $165,000 to a company owned by the Toronto Railway Company.[45] The Sisters used this financial windfall to pursue new activities elsewhere in Toronto, and they remain an important provider of health and social services in the city to the present day.

The Toronto Railway Company had no intention of growing vegetables or grazing livestock on its farm. With its lease on Munro Park soon to expire and, not yet ready to abandon the amusement park business, it needed a place to build a replacement, and the size and location of the House of Providence farm made it ideal. And of course, a large block of land in a rapidly growing neighbourhood was a solid investment. The company acquired title to the entire property, which included the beach and the "water lot" that extended into the lake (see chapter 6), and immediately set to work building its amusement park and, perhaps unwittingly, removing the last vestiges of farming in the district. It opened its elaborate new facility in the summer of 1907 under the name Scarboro Beach Amusement Park, using the simplified, phonetic spelling of the adjacent Ontario township (and the ancient English town).

Scarboro Beach was not unlike what Munro Park had been for ten years, but on a much larger scale.[46] Modelled directly after Luna Park on Coney Island, which had opened in 1903, its central feature, as at Luna Park, was a Shoot the Chutes ride in which flat boats slid down a watery ramp into a pool of water with an exhilarating splash. But it also offered professional team sports (on a large playing field), bicycle races (on a wood-floored velodrome), stage shows, dining and dancing, and no end of circus-style amusements – all powered and lit by electricity, of course, which the Toronto Railway Company had in good supply (figure 22). Electric companies, street railways, and amusement parks were a common business triad in North America in these years.[47] Amusement parks consumed electricity, as did street railways, and the more (fare-paying) customers the railways brought to the (admission-charging) amusements the more electricity the electric companies sold. It was a highly profitable arrangement, made secure by the monopolies that electric and street railway companies usually had with the cities they served.

Figure 22. In addition to the standard amusement park attractions (above) Scarboro Beach also had areas for athletic competitions (below) with ample seating for spectators. The two children, likely drawn to the photographer's tripod, are enjoying the park in 1907, the first year of its operation; the cyclists on the velodrome are competing in either 1924 or 1925, the latter being its final year.

City of Toronto Archives (Fonds 1244, Items 184A (above) and 8167)

Scarboro Beach Amusement Park operated for nineteen years, from 1907 to 1925, attracting thousands of visitors, day after day, summer after summer. There are probably more photographs of it in its heyday than of any other place or period in the neighbourhood's history. Yet for all this popularity and visibility the park's activities seem to have been rather detached from the neighbourhood around it. It was, as the earlier amusement parks had been, an "attraction" meant to draw people from elsewhere. Balmy Beach residents are said to have paddled their canoes into positions offshore to hear Sunday night orchestra performances for free; how often they or other neighbourhood residents paid an admission price to get the full experience is open to speculation.[48] Balmy Beach residents apparently viewed the park's predecessor, Munro Park, more as a source of noise than of pleasure, and as something to endure rather than enjoy.[49] No doubt similar sentiments existed about this bigger enterprise.

The park began falling out of favour in the 1920s, as did similar attractions in other cities, victims of changing tastes and greater use of automobiles. By this time, the Toronto Railway Company itself was defunct, having been effectively put out of business in 1921 when the City created the municipally run Toronto Transportation Commission to operate the street railway. The company closed Scarboro Beach for good in 1925 and added the park's land and equipment to its long list of assets under liquidation.[50] Rather curiously, considering the park's nearly two decades of operation, almost no trace of it remains on the neighbourhood landscape. The only real remnant is the location and name of Scarborough Beach Boulevard (traditional spelling restored), which began life as the roadway from Queen Street to the park's main gate. Standing at the park's site now one is hard pressed to imagine it ever existing, notwithstanding the historical plaque saying that it did. Soon after it closed, and its substantial structures were cleared away, its site was covered with housing, some of it in a form that became and remains a distinctive feature of the neighbourhood.

The park property emerged from the railway company's liquidation in the hands of the Provident Investment Company. Exactly how this came about is not clear. A newspaper reported that Provident paid $290,000 for the entire site, which the City assessed that year at about $390,000; land transaction records, however, show ownership being transferred to Provident for one dollar.[51] Provident, through its founder, A.E. Cox, had long been associated with the railway company and this transfer might have been some sort of reconciliation of investments and debts between them. Provident was, of course, actively developing Stewart Manor on the other side of Queen Street, so it was well suited to do with the land what the street railway probably assumed it would do some day – use it for residential development. Provident wasted no time. In September 1925, it registered a plan of subdivision carving the site into some 200 residential building lots.[52]

Most of the lots were fifty feet wide, customary by this time, and all look to have been bought, again following custom, by local builders intending to put houses on them, which they did without delay.[53] By September 1926, builders had fifty houses for sale. Provident's development process was here more akin to that of the prewar subdividers than to how it built up Stewart Manor, with which it obviously did not want to compete. It imposed no size or design restrictions. Houses were all of brick, but that was the builders' choice, not Provident's requirement. Most builders put two buildings on each fifty-foot lot, a good many of them side-by-side (semi-detached) duplexes.[54] This was no exclusive enclave. It was like the rest of the Beaches – an area of modest, well-built houses on small lots that could serve as homes for people of modest means. In fact, the greatest number of lots was purchased by an established local builder, Price Brothers, whose building superintendent, Harry Stevens, devised a distinctive two-storey "fourplex" with four single-floor, multi-bedroom flats, two up and two down, running front to back, each with its own small front porch – perhaps a nod to the lakefront houses a few blocks away. Price Brothers built dozens of these structures, some with Spanish colonial details, along Scarborough Beach Boulevard and the north-south streets either side of it, Glen Manor and Hammersmith, as well as a few on Queen Street (figure 23). The company retained ownership of most of what it built, at first anyway, equipping the flats with appliances and offering them for rent.[55]

The upshot was that within only a few years this erstwhile amusement park property was covered with a residential fabric as dense as, if not denser than, what stood either side of it. The detached houses were squeezed in tightly enough, but the fourplexes, each of which covered a large proportion of the lot they were on, effectively placed four households on a single fifty-foot lot. And the final stages of this project saw several rental apartment buildings erected along its northern

Figure 23. Price brothers Leslie (right) and E. Stanley stand either side of their father Joseph, president and founder of the firm, with their distinctive "fourplex" housing under construction behind them.

The Globe, 2 July 1928, p. 11; courtesy of Toronto Public Library, Special Collections

and southern borders.[56] With no city plan or planner requiring that builders not exceed a certain "floor space index," as would be the case today, builders were free to build as they wished, or, to put it another way, free to build what they thought would yield the greatest revenue or profit.[57]

Given how readily Price Brothers conceived and erected their multi-unit rental buildings, and how many small semi-detached houses the other builders put up, it seems possible that Provident was encouraging builders to make low-cost and rental housing, perhaps as a counterpoise, or complement, to Stewart Manor. There is no evidence of explicit, top-down direction, but the builders must have been working with an understanding that such housing was desirable or, at the very least, permitted. This is understandable considering that Provident's president, A.H. Cox, along with his partners, was building other multi-unit buildings in the Beaches, including Kew Beach Mansions (see below).[58] And as Henry Ford had shown not many years before, in the new consumer society there was more money to be made producing a large number of inexpensive things than a small number of expensive ones. The Scarboro Beach redevelopment did not employ modern planning and design, but in its large scale, its inexpensive products, and its rapid and efficient construction, along with a degree of mass-produced uniformity in what was built, it signalled the advent of modern development practices as much as Stewart Manor did (figure 24).

***

One other important element of the neighbourhood's physical landscape took shape in the interwar years: the distinctive character of its main commercial thoroughfare, Queen Street. Like so much else in the neighbourhood, the street's mature form was largely a product of private enterprise, although in this case private enterprise acting within, or perhaps more correctly in response to, municipal government constraints.

Queen Street had become a full-fledged street only after Toronto annexed it in 1887 and subsequently realigned it according to a proper survey and upgraded it to city

Figure 24. Nearly an entire block of newly completed Price Brothers "fourplexes" along the west side of Glen Manor Road, c. 1926.

City of Toronto Archives (Fonds 1034, Item 69)

standards. Municipal authorities at the time seem to have given no thought to how the street would function as the neighbourhood grew, and they imposed no land-use or lot-size restrictions on streetside property for there was no legal basis for doing so. Plans of subdivision that included Queen Street usually laid out the lots that fronted Queen slightly differently from those elsewhere – narrower, or shallower – and sometimes with a block-long laneway behind them to facilitate deliveries to and from businesses. Subdividers could see where the street was headed and drew their plans accordingly, but nothing compelled them to do this.

Moreover, with nothing designating lots as either residential or commercial, the street acquired a mix of both; some builders put up houses, often quite substantial houses with porches and front yards, while others put up commercial buildings, mostly utilitarian brick structures extending right to the sidewalk, to be leased to shop owners or service providers. There was a demand for both residential and commercial buildings on the street, so both were supplied. Toronto streets had been built up this way for years.

But in the 1920s, with the neighbourhood's growing population having money to spend and more and more local businesses offering goods and services for sale, Queen Street became predominantly a shopping street, and with this came a rising demand for premises where sellers could set up a shop. Responding to this, some residential property owners put additions on the fronts of their buildings, extending their houses forward to the sidewalk to create accessible, and they hoped profitably leasable, commercial space. The result was a curious, sometimes rather jerry-built, type of commercial building with a plain but practical single-storey structure grafted on the front of an older, usually two-storey, wooden-clad house. This was certainly not prescribed, but neither was it proscribed, and dozens of property owners did it. Several of these structures stand on Queen Street to this day housing shops of various sorts (figure 25).

It was in the 1920s, as well, that the eastern half of Queen Street came to be lined with apartment buildings. Toronto homeowners had been trying to keep apartments out of their residential neighbourhoods since that form of

Figure 25. Upper image is a 1903 photograph of a private residence, southeast corner of Queen Street and Waverley Road, built 1901, noteworthy for being a residential property on Queen Street as well as a shingled, cottage-style year-round home. As of 1926 (pictured here 1935) it was occupied, and probably owned, by the commercial florist J. Heywood, who added the forward extension – well-endowed with windows to display his flowers.

Upper: Courtesy of Toronto Public Library (LOCHIST-BE-026); Lower: City of Toronto Archives (Fonds 1035, Item 165) housing first appeared in the city in the 1890s. This opposition had grown strong enough to produce, in 1912, a city bylaw prohibiting apartment buildings on most residential streets.[59] This bylaw had had minimal impact on the Beaches, already largely built up by 1912, but it was still in effect in the 1920s.

The bylaw's prohibition did not apply to major thoroughfares. Nothing in the bylaw explicitly states this, but the long list of streets to which the prohibition applied – which runs for pages – includes no major through street. Not surprisingly, considering the strong demand for housing in 1920s Toronto, the bylaw yielded plenty of what it did not disallow – apartment buildings on through streets. This might not have been the intention of the bylaw, but it was undoubtedly a consequence of it, surely no surprise to anyone familiar with Toronto real estate at the time. Toronto still has countless early twentieth-century apartment buildings on its major through streets. An intriguing aspect of this is that since streetcars often ran on these streets Toronto ended up with most of its earliest apartment buildings well served by public transit. Present-day planning policies encourage and sometimes even prescribe this sort of relationship between higher-density housing and public transit, usually under the name "transit-oriented development." Interestingly, it appeared here in 1920s Toronto not because it was prescribed, yet neither was it a product of unregulated market forces; it was the market's response to the city's regulation of the market.

One of the more striking examples of this Toronto-wide phenomenon is in the Beaches, where, in the 1920s, builders erected numerous apartment buildings along Queen Street east from Lee Avenue. In some cases, builders demolished old wooden structures to make way for them, while in others, particularly further east, apartment buildings look to have been the first substantial structures on unbuilt lots. The first, and most elegant, was the fifteen-suite Kew Beach Mansions, built by the firm Cox and Best in 1926 on the southwest corner of Queen and Lee Avenue. Cox was still the head of Provident Investments and deeply involved in both the Stewart Manor and the Scarboro Beach developments, but he was also active as both an independent small-scale developer and a construction contractor.[60] In some capacity he or Provident was involved in the construction of apartment buildings along the Queen Street edge of the Scarboro Beach redevelopment, among them buildings named, unsurprisingly, Glen Manor and Stewart Manor.

Apartment buildings appeared elsewhere in the neighbourhood too, not just on Queen Street. The prohibition against their construction was evidently far from ironclad.[61] A property owner wanting to build an apartment building on a site where they were not permitted did have to obtain a site-specific amendment to the bylaw, but this seems to have been easy enough to do. Kew Beach Mansions, for example, which although primarily on Queen Street also occupied lots around the corner along residential Lee Avenue, where apartment buildings were not allowed, so Cox and Best requested that the bylaw be amended to permit their building and their request was promptly granted.[62] Not all requests came from builders with the pedigree or the connections of

A.H. Cox. Some came from ordinary homeowners seeking permission to convert part of their house into rentable flats; others came from small-scale builders intending to build an actual apartment house, with maybe ten or more suites. Most of these were granted as well.[63]

Responsibility for evaluating the applications lay with the City Building Commissioner, who, before coming to a decision, wrote letters to nearby residents requesting their views on the proposed building – an early form of public consultation. The Commissioner's inquiries nearly always uncovered some opposition, but the majority usually did not reply, and this indifference led to the Commissioner being unwilling to turn down the application.[64] In his mind, if the majority of those polled did not express opposition, the building should be allowed. One such case was a request by local builder George L. Gardiner for permission to build a twenty-suite apartment house on lakefront property he owned east of Silver Birch Avenue, where some old frame buildings stood at the time. The Commissioner wrote to thirty-five adjacent residents. Seventeen replied, of which all but two opposed it; but since eighteen did not reply that meant opponents were less than half of those polled (fifteen opposed, twenty not opposed) so the Commissioner approved the building – with a proviso that Gardiner not build the garage he had in his sketch. The apartment building stands to this day, without a garage.[65]

CHAPTER SIX

The Lost Beach

The interwar years also saw the creation of what may now be the best-known element of the entire neighbourhood – the sandy beaches, grassy picnic areas, and kilometres-long boardwalk of Beaches waterfront park. This iconic public space was established over the course of some twenty years, starting with halting efforts by the federally appointed Toronto Harbour Commissioners and concluding with the decisive actions of the City of Toronto in what is surely the boldest commandeering of private into public property in the neighbourhood's history. The park's creation profoundly disturbed the neighbourhood. It might have represented the greatest good for the greatest number, but it did not look that way in the eyes of many locals.[1] The neighbourhood's semi-private cottage community, though reduced to a lakefront margin by decades of residential development, still existed through the 1920s. By 1931 it was gone.

***

The idea of a public park along the eastern beaches had been in the air for years, but the first step towards actually creating one came in 1912 when the Toronto Harbour Commissioners, a body formed by the government of Canada just the previous year, came forward with a sweeping plan to remake the city's entire waterfront with new commercial, industrial, and recreational facilities.[2] The largest, and ultimately most consequential, component of this plan was filling in Ashbridge's Bay marsh and building an extensive new industrial precinct on the land so created. This massive undertaking would preoccupy the Commissioners for much of the 1920s and change the city's central waterfront forever.[3] But the eastern beaches, as they were labelled, were part of the scheme too. The plan's text scarcely mentions them but its main map, which depicts the scheme from city limit to city limit, shows a new breakwater running along their entire length, and the formal transfer of City-owned waterfront land to the Commissioners, effected the year the plan was released, included land as far east as the Scarboro Beach Amusement Park.[4] So the eastern beaches were, formally at least, part of the Commissioners' waterfront domain from the start, even though the Commissioners appear to have had no clear idea what to do with them.

Matters would remain at a standstill for some time. A plan was prepared in 1912 – whether done for the City or the Commissioners is not clear – calling for some sort of boulevard along the eastern beaches, and it appears to have been revised the following year, but nothing came of this early work.[5] Not until late 1920, some ten years after the main plan's release, did the Commissioners take concrete steps towards developing the eastern waterfront, announcing that year their intention to create "a recreational amusement area in the east end between Woodbine Avenue and Victoria Park" that would include "a breakwater, anchorage harbour for pleasure craft, boathouses, refreshment booths and a pavilion, together with a 20-foot promenade."[6] These "plans," as the Commissioners called them, were likely not very well developed (the City referred to them as "sketches") but their preparation and release signalled that something was underway.[7]

They also brought to light the obstacle that had been impeding progress all these years – the private ownership of waterfront properties and associated "water lots," all of which were essential for any public park (water lots are land under water, usually extending several hundred feet from shore, permitting owners to dredge harbours and construct docks).[8] Woodbine Beach, the sandy eastern border of the Ashbridge's Bay marsh that projected into the lake from the west end of the Beaches, posed the least trouble in this regard. The government of Canada had transferred ownership of that marshland, including its beach border, to the City in 1880.[9] Some years later the City began leasing lots there to individuals, who built small cottages, but it never relinquished ownership of the land, so in 1911, when it transferred all municipal waterfront property to the Harbour Commissioners, the Woodbine Beach lots were part of that transfer.[10] Transferring the land did not extinguish the leases. There were maybe one hundred leaseholders at the time, and the Commissioners would have to deal with them and their cottages in due course, but Woodbine Beach had no private owners.[11]

The beach in front of the Beaches neighbourhood, however, had scores of private owners and a complex patchwork of ownership that defied easy resolution. Some private holdings were large and some were small, some owners were recent and some long-standing, some had built structures on the beach and some had not, and some had leased their land to others.[12] Waterfront lots generally included the beach out to the water's edge, although for lessees this was not always the case (figure 26). The City owned some of the water lots. It had acquired the water lot in front of Kew Gardens when it purchased the property, which like most long-standing holdings included the associated water lot, but east and west of the park it owned only the water lots in front of the streets, not the cottages.[13] The Toronto Railway Company owned the huge water lot in front of Scarboro Beach Amusement Park; it had been attached to the farm property the company bought in 1906.[14] Many of the Balmy Beach water lots were still held by the estates or heirs of Adam Wilson's partners. Converting all this to public property was an administrative challenge of the first order, but it would have to be done.

Council passed one expropriation bylaw in 1920 and another a year later revising the boundaries slightly.[15] Both explicitly excluded the Toronto Railway Company's beach and its water lot; the City offered to buy both, but the company refused – what would their amusement park be without its lakefront?[16] This refusal, together with the City's reluctance to expropriate a viable and popular business, stymied progress for several more years. A public waterfront park was simply not possible with a large block of private

Figure 26. Looking west along Kew Beach at Kenilworth Avenue, 22 April 1918. Was this a public or a private beach?

City of Toronto Archives (Fonds 1231, Item 933)

land in the middle of it. The demise of the amusement park in 1925 and the associated liquidation of the railway company's assets put everything in a new light, although not entirely to the City's advantage. As recounted above, immediately after Provident Investment acquired the amusement park property it had registered a plan of subdivision for it, the beach and water lot still included. But the last thing the City wanted was a new residential enclave with its own beach and lake access – that would debase the public park even more than the amusement park would have – so it immediately stepped in and bought the beach and water lot from Provident. It paid a premium, nearly twice what it had offered the railway company five years earlier, but circumstances compelled the City to pay what Provident asked.

By 1925 the land for the waterfront park was all in public hands, or at least all in the process of becoming so – several former owners were disputing what the City had paid them for their property, and arbitrations were holding up formal transfer.[17] But the Harbour Commissioners were not making much headway either, perhaps understandable given the magnitude of their new Toronto Industrial District, as they had named the Ashbridge's Bay infill. They did manage to evict Woodbine Beach cottagers whose leases had expired, many of whom, as a final act of defiance, left behind dilapidated cottages.[18] The Commissioners also began dredging the lake bottom in 1929 in preparation for building breakwaters and harbour facilities, although they seem to have made little progress on this work.[19]

At some point through all this delay the City resolved to finish the job itself, and in doing so shifted the focus from water to land.[20] The City had no desire for breakwaters and anchorages; it just wanted a better beach, and to achieve this it opted to build more short, low piers, or groynes, at right angles to the shore that would impede water movement and thus encourage sand deposit. It had begun this on a small scale twenty years earlier, with some success.[21] These unbeautiful structures debased the beach somewhat, giving it something of an industrial-harbour look, but they worked; so more were built, and the beach did indeed begin growing out into the lake. The Harbour Commissioners appear not to have objected to the City doing this work. In fact, they seem to have essentially abandoned responsibility for improving the eastern beaches, announcing in 1929 that any further work they did there would be billed to the City, at costs plus 10 per cent.[22]

The City also opted to expropriate more land, its first step in this direction being to take a strip of property from Provident's new subdivision, an action prompted by unusual circumstances. The plan of subdivision that Provident had registered in 1925, after the City bought the beach and water lots, had eighteen residential lots along the southern property line, as close to the now City-owned beach as permissible; these lots fronted on a new residential street named Hubbard Boulevard and backed against the beach. Provident began selling them in 1927, and the westernmost four were immediately bought by a known local builder.[23] Even a cursory look at the plan of subdivision would have revealed that houses built on these lots, though fronting on Hubbard, would be effectively on the beach, so the City was concerned (figure 27). It was prepared to leave *existing* lakefront cottages intact – to this point it had expropriated just beach, not inshore property – but *new* lakefront housing it certainly did not want. It did nothing to stop this builder, for the owner of the lots had every right to put up houses on them, and likely had already taken preliminary steps to do so. But the City could, and did, do something to halt any further lakefront house building – in September 1927 it expropriated the remaining fourteen lots in that southernmost strip with the intention of incorporating them into the park.[24]

The owner of the four lots began building promptly, and by mid-1928 had erected five structures: three fourplexes, one detached house, and one apartment building. It was probably the sort of housing that City authorities had expected, for it is what was being built elsewhere in the new development. But what the City might not have expected is that the owner/builders, with no restrictions on where to put front and back doors on what they built, had

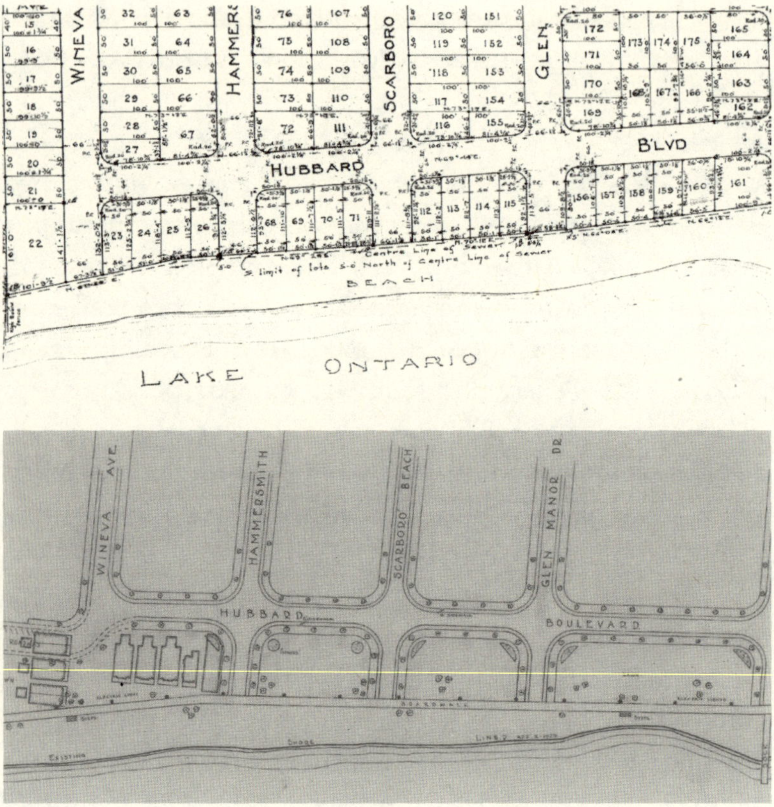

Figure 27. Southern portion of Provident Investments' 1925 plan of subdivision (upper) for the amusement park property, with eighteen lots on the south side of Hubbard Boulevard, and the same property in the City's 1931 plan for Eastern Beaches Park, showing houses on lots 23–26 (and on lot 22, facing Wineva Avenue) but parkland on all lots to the east.

Upper: Registered Plan of Subdivision #M490, 26 November 1925 (Ontario Land Registry Records); Lower: "Proposed Improvements Eastern Beaches," 1 June 1931, City of Toronto Archives (Series 724, Item 291) put porches and front doors on the backs of their houses and garages and back doors on the fronts, producing a run of new buildings which, although addressed on Hubbard Boulevard, was truly, unmistakably on the beach – exactly what the City did not want. The City had clearly been outfoxed. This rather amusing chain of events might have embarrassed a few municipal officials – though there is no evidence of this – but more importantly it showed the City that the beach alone, without any adjacent inshore land, was insufficient for a true public park. This recognition, and the additional expropriation that resulted, turned out to be the first step in a major expansion of the park (figure 27).

Soon after this the City began working to acquire a block of what looks to have been marshy land in a residential part of Kew Beach as a site for a new athletic field thought to be needed since the closure of the amusement park's field.[25] But a much greater addition of parkland followed a year later, in 1930, when the City resolved to expropriate a strip of inshore property along the full length of the park, essentially to do what it had done along Hubbard Boulevard for the entire beach, and to clear away nearly every structure on it, effectively doubling the park's area.[26] This removal of perhaps a hundred privately owned buildings – cottages, boathouses, boarding houses, hotels – was nothing short of cataclysmic for the neighbourhood. Some of the cottages, especially those in the western part of Kew Beach, were rather crude structures, without foundations, and probably not long for this world, but several on the Balmy Beach waterfront were substantial.[27] Among the houses demolished were those of the early patrician cottagers who had founded the Balmy Beach community – Snow, Beaty, Lumbers, and even Adam

Figure 28. Cottage of A.J. Russell Snow (b. 1859), 11 September 1930, prior to its expropriation and demolition. Snow built this cottage c. 1895 at the foot of Balsam Avenue, east side, facing west rather than south towards the lake. He was living in Toronto in 1930, with his family, but the cottage appears to be no longer in use.

City of Toronto Archives (Series 372, Sub-series 3, Item 892)

Wilson. Signs are that these original cottages were no longer being maintained and were destined for demolition, but even so it was a major, and sudden, loss (figure 28).

The neighbourhood was profoundly unsettled. The hundred or so displaced cottage owners were the most upset, of course, and unlikely ever to vote for the city politicians who had pushed this through. But residents farther away from the lake were affected too, for many of them still used the beach – *their* beach as they would have seen it. The City had its reasons for doing what it did. Not only were many waterfront buildings structurally unsound and unlikely to last much longer, those along the western section, where there was no bank, were vulnerable to water damage when lake levels rose, and the City, as owner of the beach, might have been responsible for this damage.[28] But perhaps most fundamentally, the City was aware that over the course of fifty-some years an ill-defined, and never truly mandated, pattern of private ownership had developed.[29] Not wanting this to continue, the City opted to eradicate it, here and now, in one fell swoop.

In considering the City's drastic action and its effect on hundreds of unhappy locals, one should not overlook the fact that tens of thousands of Toronto residents would now have greater access to the eastern waterfront. The City had reclaimed the beach for the public. But neither can one overlook that the City, in doing what it did, removed a piece of neighbourhood history. This, surely, was not its intention. Its objective was to remove the present and secure the future, not eradicate the past; nevertheless, by clearing away nearly all physical evidence of an important chapter of Beaches history, the City did just that. Indeed, in the absence of any physical evidence, few park users – even local residents with some knowledge of neighbourhood history – are aware that the strip of grassy land alongside the beach was once covered, from one end of the park to the other, by private cottages and boathouses.

The new Eastern Beaches Waterfront Park opened on Victoria Day 1932, with some 60,000 visitors attending the parade, speeches, and athletic events that marked the occasion.[30] The new park was, in truth, nothing special. The City had steered clear of creative design, as it had for Kew Gardens twenty-five years earlier, and devised a perfectly serviceable, readily constructed, and doubtless inexpensive city park, the plan for which was undersigned not by any notable landscape designer but by the Commissioner of Parks.[31] There was no major landscaping or building, just a continuous swath of level green space alongside the now unmistakably public beach, a public boardwalk running the full length of that green space, and an athletic field carved out of an old residential part of Kew Beach. It was unlikely to win any design awards, but it was a big step forward for Toronto's public realm (figure 29).

Keeping with the pragmatism of the undertaking, the park excluded three stretches of waterfront property. One was the block of housing that had sparked expropriation of the adjacent beachfront lots in 1927. These structures – in the end, six pairs of semi-detached houses (three facing Wineva) plus the detached house and apartment building – had been expropriated in 1930 and were slated for demolition along with all the other private properties, but since they were just a few years old and well built, the City opted to retain and lease them, turning them into modest revenue producers.[32] So the City became landlord of the houses it had not wanted, and a small group of private residences remained on the beach after all, publicly owned but privately occupied (see figure 27). The Balmy Beach Club clubhouse also survived. The terms of East Toronto's annexation had given the club permission to occupy its site, and the City, thinking those terms might stand in the way of expropriation, held back. The Club's members offered to allow the City to rebuild their clubhouse – at the City's expense, estimated at $86,000 – so as to permit the new public boardwalk to run through Balmy Beach Park, but the City thought not. The boardwalk stopped where the old clubhouse remained.[33]

Figure 29. Beaches Park, looking east from Waverley Road, 5 August 1931. The park was not officially opened for another year (Victoria Day 1932), and the boardwalk did not yet have its boards, but clearly the beach had already been transformed into a public space.

City of Toronto Archives (Series 372, Sub-series 52, Item 1481)

The private properties east of Silver Birch Avenue also remained. The original plan had been for the park to extend to the eastern city limit, several hundred metres east of Balmy Beach Park, and the 1920 bylaw had expropriated the beach and water lots out to that point. But the 1930 bylaw expropriating the additional inshore property had stopped at Silver Birch, perhaps because some of the buildings east of there also were new. In 1931, before completing the park, the City considered taking this land, but the estimated heavy cost, $750,000, gave council a case of cold feet from which it never recovered.[34] This stretch of housing, which includes the twenty-suite apartment building mentioned above, is one of the few places in Toronto with private housing directly on the public (on account of earlier expropriation) beach. The City surely never imagined the permanence of its decisions, but nearly a hundred years later these three patches of private property – the newly built houses, the Balmy Beach Club, and everything east of Silver Birch – remain excluded from the public park.

***

A little over a year after it opened, the park was the site of dramatic events that have drawn considerable attention over the years – a brief, startling flash of antisemitism. The story has been told so many times – it has even been fictionalized[35] – that another telling might seem superfluous. But when recounted as an episode in the history of the neighbourhood rather than the history of antisemitism, its usual context, it looks quite different, and becomes more understandable.[36] That is not to suggest anti-semitism was absent – it is unmissable – but to point out that local circumstances were also at work. While one might question whether these events are central to the neighbourhood's history, the neighbourhood's history was undoubtedly central to these events.

They occurred over the course of a single week in early August 1933.[37] The new park was being overrun with visitors that summer; literally thousands were coming out to swim and picnic by day and stroll the boardwalk by night. The busiest areas were generally at Kew Gardens and along Kew Beach, where the gala opening had been held the previous year, but crowds spilled east to what the Balmy Beach

Club still considered to be (but in fact no longer was) its own waterfront. Non-members, almost certainly unaware that the clubhouse was a private facility, were known to have entered it to change into bathing attire, and some of these visitors, when discovered, had apparently been ushered out rather roughly. Locals began pointing out that these interlopers were Jews – some probably were – and soon a whisper campaign developed to keep Jews off the beach. Signs began appearing in the form of swastikas painted on rocks (quickly erased by authorities so we have no visual evidence) and small swastika badges on sleeves. Sometime in late July a letter was posted on the Balmy Beach Club's bulletin board, undersigned by "a group of beach residents," asking for help ridding the beach of "undesirables."[38]

The situation came into sharper focus on 1 August, when placards painted with swastikas were mounted on poles outside the club, at least one with "Hail Hitler" handprinted beside the pattern, and a second letter was posted inside, this one undersigned by a group calling itself "Local 5 of the Swastika Committee, Kew Beach" (figure 30).[39] The letter asked Balmy Beach Club members to buy a swastika badge for twenty-five cents and join Kew Beach committee members in nightly parades along the boardwalk to keep the "undesirables" in their place. It was not clear who or what was behind this campaign or, for that matter, what specifically it was trying to accomplish. The Balmy Beach Club claimed innocence, which is probably true for the institution but clearly not for all its members.

A prominent display of swastikas in front of the Balmy Beach Club, a nationally recognized amateur sporting

Figure 30. First public reporting of the Swastika incident, showing the placard mounted on a post in front of the Balmy Beach Club.

The Evening Telegram, 1 August 1933; courtesy of Toronto Public Library, Special Collections

institution, was a newsworthy event, and local papers responded as one would expect. Late the next evening after thirty or forty "Swastikas," as they were being called, had completed their parade up and down the boardwalk, a well-travelled, streetwise Jewish tough named Al Kaufman arrived with the "Uptown Gang" of fifty or sixty young Jewish men – all in one transport truck apparently – to assert a Jewish presence and investigate. With Kaufman out front led by a large, leashed dog they paraded to and around the Balmy Beach clubhouse, mingling with club members and looking for antisemitic displays. They found none, for the signs had been removed, and no trouble ensued. Their actions, however, attracted hundreds of young people, prompting the club manager to call the police who, when they arrived, advised the club to terminate the dance underway inside, which it did – the band played "God Save the King" to usher the dancers out. By midnight police had dispersed the crowd and Kaufman and his gang had walked back to their truck and departed. Then the Swastikas, stirred to action, reassembled and began another march along the boardwalk, at one point singing a crude antisemitic song; some two hundred initially joined the march but numbers fell off as it proceeded. Observers noted with a good deal of relief that the Swastika Committee and the Uptown Gang had not crossed paths.

Newspapers reported all this quite prominently, and word spread. Everyone was shocked. The affair seems to have come out of the blue. Who were these Swastikas? What was going on? Nobody knew, and in fact much remains unknown to this day. We know they were young locals, nearly all male, but we do not know what they thought about Jews, what if anything they knew about international affairs, or how numerous they were. Nor do we know if they anticipated how their actions would be received. Displaying swastikas and parading against "undesirables," in 1933, in a city with a large Jewish population, was not going to be seen as a harmless prank by informed people. Indeed, it was not. It drew fervid criticism from all quarters – city councillors, Jewish community spokesmen, Protestant churchmen, even the mayor, all issued public condemnations the next day. Rabbi Samuel Sachs declared their actions "beneath contempt" and announced that the League for the Defence of Jewish Rights, of which he was chairman, would immediately investigate; Meyer Steinglass, managing editor of *The Jewish Standard* stated that the swastika signs were threats "not merely to Jewish rights but to the democratic rights of all Canadians."[40]

The Swastikas, for their part, remained aloof and evasive. They gave no names, spoke vaguely about their organization, and denied being antisemitic – they were just "Beach residents who want to keep the beaches clean and nice."[41] And they toyed with reporters' questions. Who is behind your movement? A mystery man. Why the swastika? For good luck. Why "Hail Hitler"? Just a joke. Where had those badges come from? Several places. *The Globe* stated that the mysterious club "is reported to have a membership of over four hundred," not citing its source, but the same article quoted the posted appeal letter saying the group had a membership of forty.[42] Labelling it Local 5 of course implied at least four others – but none had been heard from. Of the two hundred paraders "many" wore swastika badges, but nobody said how many.

The Swastikas kept up nightly parades along the crowded boardwalk, apparently causing no trouble, but they also became better organized, naming two members as spokesmen – Bert Ganter and Harold Mackay – and announcing their objective: "by assisting the civic authorities to exclude from their district all obnoxious and undesirable elements who tend to destroy the natural beauty and property value of the residential districts of Toronto," with no mention of Jews.[43] After some reflection Jewish spokesmen responded with a public statement: this protest was an insignificant event, they had concluded, carried out by youngsters, and maybe should just be ignored, but their use of the swastika was worrisome since it suggested links to other, more nefarious, groups. The mayor proposed a meeting between the Swastikas and Jewish leaders, but the Swastikas turned him down.

The main event occurred a few days later, on the Sunday of the Civic Holiday weekend, with the park and boardwalk crammed with visitors. Jewish social groups were in the habit of organizing large day-long picnics along the beach and this holiday weekend was no exception; some three thousand Jewish picnickers were expected. The organizing body considered cancelling the picnics in light of recent events, but resolved to proceed, declaring that their picnickers would have "full police protection and no right-minded Canadian will interfere with them if they behave themselves as good citizens."[44] They arranged for a group of Jewish boys "of the better element" – presumably not the Uptown Boys – to patrol the beach and make sure Jewish picnickers did not disturb or provoke. The Swastikas promised to be out in full force too. So did the police.

Conflict began with the Swastikas drawing jeers and insults from the crowd as they moved about in small groups flaunting swastikas printed on their badges and painted on their sweatshirts. After several hours of this the police inspector in charge, showing no sympathy for the Swastikas and determined to defuse tensions, began pulling the badges off their arms. This led to a confrontation with the two leaders. The inspector demanded they remove their shirts, but they refused. Crowds began chanting for removal of the shirts until a "large Jewish man" stepped forward and tried to rip the shirt off one of them, landing a punch in the process, and several other fist fights broke out. After quelling the fights, a police inspector guided the two leaders into a nearby boathouse and declared he would not let them out until they removed their shirts – treating them rather like schoolboys – but still they refused. The two remained in informal detention for a half hour until finally, after some negotiations, they relented "and with their sweatshirts rolled up under their arms made their way unmolested down the boardwalk."[45] The drama was over (figure 31).

Early the next week, the two Swastika leaders, Ganter and Mackay, accepted the mayor's invitation to a meeting that would include senior representatives of several Jewish groups, the mayor and some councillors, the president of the Balmy Beach Club, and a man representing the neighbourhood homeowners – a theretofore unreported voice in the affair. The main spokesmen for the Swastikas, Bert Ganter, had three points to make: the beach and its facilities were being overused and degraded, his committee was more intent on saving the beach than keeping out Jews, and he and his confreres had not known the significance of the swastika symbol to Jewish people. In response to the last of these Rabbi Sachs explained, with a gravity that must have unsettled the young men, "to Jewish people today the swastika is the symbol of a wild beast crouching over 600,000 people, sucking their blood," and he went on to say, in response to the second, "if you are sincere in your desire to keep the beaches clean, what about the broom as a symbol?"[46]

On Ganter's first point the Jewish spokesmen had little to say but the homeowners' representative had plenty. The beach had been essentially taken over by day visitors from the city,

Figure 31. Hundreds of park visitors, no doubt drawn by the name-calling and fistfights, crowd around the boathouse, 7 August 1933. The officer in charge was likely holding the two troublemakers inside the boathouse at this very moment, for the photographer would have been closely following the drama.

City of Toronto Archives (Globe and Mail Fonds, Fonds 1266, Item 30688)

he explained. Truckloads, literally, of people were arriving on weekend mornings, and many were changing into swimsuits in the uncovered backs of the trucks, some right in the open air. Large groups of picnickers were leaving refuse in the park and along streets near the beach. Locals were basically unable to use the park. On the climactic Sunday, a local softball team had arrived to play an organized game at the athletic field, well away from the crowded boardwalk, and found the bleachers fully occupied by picnickers with no interest in softball, and league officials had to dislodge them before the game could begin. The problems were real, he maintained, and local anger was growing. Not all the interlopers were Jews, he hastened to say; "we have objectionable people among our Canadian-born as well as those from Europe and the British Isles."[47] The Balmy Beach Club president added his voice to this point: it was the immodest swimsuit changes, the overwhelming numbers, and the careless garbage disposal that irked his members, not the religion of the individuals.

Yet the fact is that Jews were far and away the largest non-British ethnic group in Toronto at this time, and they were coming, even being brought by busloads, to the beach in large numbers.[48] Beaches residents may well have been more unsettled than they acknowledged, or realized, by the presence of so many non-Christians, for in among complaints about crowds are comments about noisy boaters not observing the Sunday Sabbath. But one must remember that the Beaches had not, until now, experienced the "foreigners" who had been immigrating into downtown and west end Toronto since the 1890s. Day-long extended family gatherings in outdoor public spaces where little English is spoken are as common in Toronto today as crowded streetcars, and widely recognized as a healthy feature in an immigrant society. But in the 1930s most residents of the Beaches had never seen such a thing.

It also appears that many of these Jewish picnickers were relatively recent immigrants, not yet acculturated to North American life.[49] At least that was the assessment of Al Kaufman, the well-travelled Jewish gang leader who had paraded around the Balmy Beach Club the first night of trouble.[50] He had stopped by again late Sunday night after the melee, on behalf of Rabbi Sachs, he claimed, this time at the Queen Street store where the Swastikas congregated. Addressing the group's two leaders, Kaufman demanded to know, reportedly in a loud voice, what this was all about. He came away convinced that the Swastikas had a point. As he put it to a reporter after his chat with the leaders, "The offenders are greenhorns from Russia. They are so glad to come to a place where the sands and waters are free to all that they go wild. When they see there are no czars they tear off all of their clothes and break the regulations, which they cannot read."[51] This was no official report, but it was candid, and although Kaufman might be accused of intergenerational prejudice he was no antisemite.

The day after the mayor's meeting the Swastikas announced they would abandon their symbol and name and redirect their efforts to conventional neighbourhood improvement. They kept their word, or at least Bert Ganter did, reconstituting their committee a few days later into the Beaches Protective Association. The association's inaugural meeting, held in a local school, was reportedly attended by some 500 residents, so evidently the wish to "protect" the beach was widely and deeply felt, and maybe dropping the offending name and emblem had made the movement palatable to more residents. Yet attendees balked at fully distancing this new association from the original club, for they felt the latter's protests had yielded noticeable improvements. A statement to this effect met with a "Chorus of Hear! Hear!"[52] So the new association, the chairman summed up, would "carry on the aims and objects of the Swastika Club in its entirety," which was "to rid the beaches of nuisances caused by Jewish, Gentile, or any other creeds in using beach property as a dressing room." But such continuity with the Swastika Club was too much for at least one Jewish resident in attendance. Mr. Morris Simkin reminded the meeting that the club's goal had been "to eliminate the Jewish people from the beach."[53] But several attendees responded to this with shouts of "no," and when the chairman countered Simkin's assertion with the challenge, "If there is anyone present with anti-Jewish feeling let him get up and leave the meeting," nobody left. This meeting, perhaps more than any other single event in the conflict, reveals the complex mix of forces – conservatism, localism, xenophobia, and antisemitism – at work.

The Swastikas' co-leader Harold Mackay had not endorsed Bert Ganter's act of conciliation. He resigned from the group and promptly became involved in more overt antisemitic activities, reminding us that at least some pure antisemitism had been present in the original committee. Only a few days later the swastika symbol would reappear to ignite the well-known "Riot at Christie Pits," confirming, should anyone need confirmation, that antisemitism was alive in the minds of at least some Torontonians. Yet despite the temporal connection there is no obvious continuity of personnel between the two events. Researchers have not found Ganter or Mackay at Christie Pits, and in fact both disappear from the historical record. Local 5 of the Kew Beach Swastika Committee was never heard from again; nor were any of the other four locals, had they ever existed. Some members of the Jewish Defence League feared the sudden eruption in the Beaches indicated connections with German Nazis – Toronto Jews were well informed about affairs in Germany.[54] This was sufficiently plausible that the *Toronto Star* wrote to Chancellor Hitler asking if it were true, and remarkably the paper received a reply: "Absurd to say Canadian anti-Jewish outbreaks in any way connected with the Nazi movement here," Ernest Hanfstaengl, official spokesman for Chancellor Hitler, replied. "The Nazi Movement is purely German and is unconnected with any other country."[55] This bizarre exchange is hardly definitive proof of anything, but it lends credence to the idea that this conflict stood on its own, free of direct international influence.[56]

All in all, it seems insufficient to view this episode as entirely an act of antisemitism, for it was so clearly bound up with neighbourhood concerns; similarly, it seems somewhat of a leap to see it as evidence that the Beaches was a particularly antisemitic place, for the conflict was so transient, and the extent to which its antisemitism was local is by no means clear. We know that antisemitism was alive in Canada at this time, and likely some antisemitic agent sparked the Kew Beach group to life, promising excitement for some – the members were consistently described as young – and neighbourhood protection for others.[57] But that spark found little fuel, and the meagre flame it ignited quickly died. Maybe some Beaches residents harboured an amorphous antisemitism, whether through ignorance or prejudice, and doubtless many residents were unfamiliar with "foreigners."[58] But they, especially those who lived close to the lake, had just lost a piece of their neighbourhood. The waterfront was not theirs anymore. Nor would it ever be. The Beaches was a Toronto neighbourhood and its waterfront a Toronto park. Surely that goes a long way towards explaining the events of August 1933.

CHAPTER SEVEN

The Neighbourhood Endures

By mid-century the neighbourhood's character was set. Its basic structure and several of its key physical elements had been in place since 1914, in the original streetcar suburb, but its full, multifarious character emerged only after the interwar additions of Stewart Manor, the Scarboro Beach Amusement Park subdivision, a fully developed commercial Queen Street lined with apartment buildings, and the Beaches Park. And this character, forged in the fifty or so years before 1940 would endure through the fifty or so years that followed, in fact into the early twenty-first century. Not that the neighbourhood remained entirely static: its social makeup changed, its population declined, its buildings aged, and it was affected by the increase in overall wealth that transformed much of urban North American after the 1960s. Yet somehow, through it all, an essential character endured. The Beaches of the 1940s is, in so many ways, the Beaches of today.

***

What was this character? How might one "characterize" the Beaches of the 1940s? First, physically, it was extremely compact. Except for its three large parks – Kew Gardens, Glen Manor, and Eastern Beaches – and its schoolyards, it was covered almost entirely with houses. Residential lots were small and most of the houses – in fact nearly every house built before 1914 – extended from lot line to lot line. Houses began being built to accommodate cars in the 1920s, some with garages incorporated into their design and some with space between adjacent houses to permit access to backyard garages by "shared driveways," as they came to be called. But neither of these innovations produced much open space. Queen Street, the main thoroughfare, was the provincially mandated sixty-six feet wide, but the City seems not to have enforced this requirement for residential streets, which were often narrower, and this added further to the neighbourhood's compactness. Apart from Stewart Manor, streets were laid out in a rectilinear grid with rectilinear houses on rectilinear lots, leaving almost no unused triangles of land. Front setbacks, which were generally (but not always) consistent, were rarely very deep, tightening the urban fabric further still (figure 32). Such density of buildings undoubtedly produced a corresponding density of population. There is no record of residential density (i.e., persons per area) but the neighbourhood in 1951 had 26,343 residents, about 7,000 separate dwellings, and thus roughly 3.8 persons per dwelling. With the density of buildings as high as it was, 3.8 persons per dwelling would have yielded considerable residential density.[1] None of this, it should be noted, was prescribed; it resulted simply from the neighbourhood's unregulated construction.

Figure 32. Aerial photograph, 1947, of the Beaches neighbourhood north of Queen Street and east of Woodbine Avenue, showing almost complete land coverage. The only unbuilt land is in the upper right – the schoolyard of Williamson Road Public School and the adjoining Ames property, but the latter, already cleared of its forest and ponds, would soon to be covered with houses like everywhere else.

City of Toronto Archives (Series 12, File 1947, Item 19F)

The small-town look of the neighbourhood – clapboard houses, absence of formal design, mixed-use main street – was another key element of its physical character.[2] The inter-war years had seen the addition of higher-quality, architect-designed houses, mostly in Stewart Manor and the extreme east end where finer houses had begun appearing even before 1914. This type of housing reflected a more affluent age, as well as a more urban mindset among land developers, builders, and presumably buyers, but confined as it was to discrete pockets it tended to expand rather than alter the neighbourhood's character. The interwar years had also seen plenty of apartment buildings added to the residential fabric; by 1951, the earliest year for which data is available, approximately one-third of the dwellings in the neighbourhood overall were classed as "apartments or flats," while south of Queen Street more than half were classed as such.[3] So the neighbourhood's housing, all told, had become more varied and more urban since 1914. Yet a small-town ambience persisted, largely because so much of it had been built before 1914, although the improvised commercial buildings on Queen Street, built after 1920, contributed to that ambience as well.

The neighbourhood's housing revealed another, less concrete but equally essential, aspect of its character: the Beaches might have been more urban by 1940, but it cannot be described as more urbane, or au courant. None of the neighbourhood's new interwar structures – houses, apartments, fourplexes, commercial buildings – show a hint of architectural modernism, or any of the new design ideas emerging in these years. Even in Stewart Manor, the neighbourhood's one truly designed district, the English "arts and crafts" architectural style employed in its housing had been in vogue for decades and was already verging on quaint when the build-out occurred in the 1920s.[4] The Price Brothers' fourplexes, an original building form that served the neighbourhood's needs and fit well in the architectural context, were innovative in their own way. Yet they did not reflect international trends in design, perfectly understandable since their "architect" was the firm's building superintendent, a gifted builder whose talents Price Brothers recognized and trusted but whose ideas were likely untouched by highbrow design fashions.[5] The Beaches of the 1940s was not a cosmopolitan or cutting-edge place. This too was integral to its character.

What can be said of the neighbourhood's social character in the 1940s? The Canadian census did not begin reporting by census tract until 1951, but since the neighbourhood seems not to have changed much between 1941 and 1951 – its 1951 population (26,704) was nearly identical to that of 1941 (26,343) – the 1951 census can serve as a reasonable stand-in for the 1940s as a decade.[6] And this census clearly reveals how little the neighbourhood's social makeup had changed since its genesis. The population was still predominantly of British origin – a census classification comprising different nationalities, including all Irish – with 82.8 per cent identifying as such; and in religious adherence its residents were still mostly Protestant Christian, the proportion of which, 81.6 per cent, closely matches that of British origin.[7] In both categories, as had been the case forty years before, the neighbourhood differed from Toronto overall, which in 1951 was 66.2 per cent British origin and 64.2 per cent Protestant Christian – the difference in religious adherence reflecting the Beaches' smaller proportion of all minority religions, but especially Roman Catholics (Beaches 13.5 per cent, Toronto 19.3 per cent).[8]

Considering the social class of residents, at least as it can be inferred from their occupations, the neighbourhood was still middle class, skewing towards working or lower middle class, and this was another key element of its social character in the 1940s.[9] The range of occupations was as wide as ever: skilled trades, clerks and managers, sales personnel and supervisors, and proprietors of small, often trades-based, businesses. Wages for such jobs probably ranged from adequate to more than adequate, and on this basis most Beaches residents in the 1940s, although by no means affluent, would have been financially self-supporting.[10] So too were they mostly hard-working, in the sense that the jobs they had would have monopolized their days and left little time, energy, or money for active leisure.

Some residents, of course, had higher-income occupations. Pine Crescent, fully built-up by 1940, was probably the most overtly posh street – some of its houses had architectural style – but the occupations of its residents hardly suggest exclusivity: chief accountant of the Presbyterian Church, metallurgist at Canada Industries Limited, department manager at Eaton's.[11] Holders of such jobs would have gone to work every day. They were upper middle class, not rich, or elite. Along with the presence of this affluence came a degree of spatial differentiation by income level, usually by street, as had been the case in the pre-1914 streetcar suburb. But social borders were by no means hard and fast; all three of the neighbourhood's public schools drew children from homes on higher and lower income streets. Stewart Manor had brought upper-middle-class residents into the neighbourhood, but at about the same time, across Queen Street, the Scarboro Beach redevelopment had introduced scores of rental units in apartment buildings and fourplexes that offered homes for lower-income or less-settled people. So the neighbourhood had a range of middle-class income levels, but a very modest, in some areas non-existent, spatial differentiation of that range.[12]

The neighbourhood was entirely residential, so nearly all employed residents had to leave the neighbourhood for their jobs.[13] Of those who worked locally, a small number worked for a local employer (manager of the local pharmacy, caretaker at the local school), and a few worked for the railway just north of the neighbourhood, now the Canadian National Railway. Some were self-employed; of these, a few actually did their paid work at home (music teacher, commercial artist), others were proprietors with no single workplace other than their home (builder) and still others – very few – were professionals with offices nearby (dentist, barrister). Taken altogether these various forms of local employment do not add up to much, roughly 2 or 3 per cent of total employment in the blocks sampled, so the neighbourhood was still largely a streetcar suburb. The employment locations of its residents had become slightly more dispersed – some now worked in the new Carlaw Street industrial district – but the majority still worked downtown, and the only realistic way to get to there, or to the

Carlaw district, was by streetcar. Automobiles had become an option in the 1930s, but only for the well off. The streetcar's continuing importance in the 1940s is perhaps most clearly revealed in the fact that in 1951 more than half the households still had no passenger car.[14]

Was the Beaches of the 1940s a neighbourhood in the social sense, a "loosely cohesive community" in the words of the dictionary definition cited in the introduction? Answering this definitively would require data on multiple social activities, and the task of finding and assembling it is beyond the scope of this study. All that can be offered here is an ambivalent answer. On one hand perhaps it was. Residents did not work in the neighbourhood, so it was not an economically cohesive community, not in the slightest, but residents did attend local schools and churches, use the neighbourhood library, and surely, considering the difficulty and cost of travelling about the city, even in these dawning days of the automobile era, shop locally as much as they could. Recollections of the few memoirists who have written about these years emphasize the community aspect: "There were few strangers in the Beach during the week," recalls Lorraine O'Donnell Williams in her memoir of growing up in the 1940s; she and her family "always saw people we knew, either by sight or by name, anywhere along Queen between Woodbine and Neville Park." The celebrated filmmaker Norman Jewison, who grew up in the neighbourhood at about the same time, offered similar recollections in an interview. Robert Fulford recalls a firm "Beacher" identity among residents.[15]

But realistically how could a population of some 26,000 be a single community, even a "loosely cohesive" one?[16]

There was no neighbourhood school – there were five – and no neighbourhood church – also five, some antagonistic to one another.[17] There was no central community public space or neighbourhood café. Nor could such a large population possibly have had a neighbourhood preacher, a neighbourhood layabout, or a neighbourhood gang of bothersome teens. Local schools and churches likely spawned "subcommunities," and these would have been important – although the school-based ones were probably evanescent, as they are today – and residents did join groups organized around specific activities.[18] But it is hard to see the Beaches overall as a single community. There had at one time been a recreational community, and the Balmy Beach Club remained an expression of that – it was very active in amateur athletics through the interwar years – but only a minority of residents were members. Children still played on the beach – everyday in the summer, Robert Fulford recalls – but it is not clear how common, or how unifying a force, swimming and boating were after the cottages and boathouses were cleared away.[19] The Beaches neighbourhood of the 1940s had a certain look, feel, and social character, but it was probably more than one community.[20]

***

"The neighbourhood, unlike us, remained the same" observes the narrator in Italian novelist Elena Ferrante's engaging portrayal of the intersecting lives of two women growing up and aging together in a postwar Naples neighbourhood.[21] Might this be true of the postwar Beaches? Did its character endure while its residents changed? One cannot approach this question too literally. A certain amount of change will occur over two generations in an immigrant-receiving city with rising standards of living, and this will affect a neighbourhood's character. Even Ferrante's narrator, later in her life, acknowledged that something about her supposedly unchanging fictional neighbourhood had changed – she calls it the "anthropological landscape" – with the arrival of non-Italian immigrants, for the people in it looked and acted differently from those she had lived among as a child.[22] Yet somehow, in real Toronto as in fictional Naples, a fundamental neighbourhood character endured. In the Beaches this is most evident in its natural setting – terrain, trees, lake – and its man-made physical elements – streets, houses, shops.[23] But aspects of its social character endured as well, leaving one to wonder if a neighbourhood's social character might persist through continuity not of its individuals, who obviously change as decades pass, but of the sort of people who choose to live in it. Does a neighbourhood retain its character by attracting and retaining those who like that character?

Little changed in the first few postwar decades. The neighbourhood's ethnic makeup, for one thing, persisted. Non-Anglos remained a minority, making the neighbourhood more and more of an outlier in the city overall.[24] While the percentage of Toronto's population classed as ethnic British fell to 51.8 per cent by 1961, and further still to 45.8 per cent by 1971, the Beaches neighbourhood held at 74.5 per cent and 73.6 per cent British in those two census years.[25] As Jim Sanderson declares in his memoir, "Our family on Kingswood Road was like many others in Balmy Beach, and as far as I was concerned this was fine."[26]

The decline of British ethnicity in Toronto overall resulted from the large number of continental European immigrants, a category which, broadly defined, reached 32.5 per cent of the city's population in 1961. But European immigrants simply did not settle in the Beaches in such numbers. Italians, for example, who flooded into Toronto by the tens of thousands beginning in the late 1950s, making the city's population 12.6 per cent ethnic Italian in 1971, were at most 2.8 per cent of the Beaches population that year (two-thirds of that 2.8 per cent resided in the most westerly census tract, only part of which is in the Beaches). As for Jews, they remained a minuscule proportion, about 0.6 per cent of the neighbourhood's population, one-tenth of their percentage in the city overall.[27] Qualitative evidence sits well with the quantitative; the Italian cafés, Portuguese bakeries, and Jewish delis integral to postwar Toronto's character rarely appear in memoirs or photographs of the Beaches. Toronto journalist Robert Fulford, who grew up in the, to him, uncosmopolitan and rather small-minded Beaches of the 1940s and 1950s, recalled, "In my public school there was exactly one Jew, in my high school there was exactly one negro (he was called 'Snowball')."[28]

This is not to suggest the neighbourhood was unwelcoming or intolerant. Expressions of antipathy towards outsiders undoubtedly did occur – most of them probably unreported and unrecorded[29] – but there is no evidence of them being more common in the Beaches than elsewhere in Toronto, notwithstanding the notorious "Swastikas" episode in August 1933. Covenants had restricted the building materials and landscaping of Stewart Manor in the 1920s and 1930s, but not the race or religion of its residents.[30] The scarcity of European immigrants in the postwar neighbourhood can be largely explained by two other factors: immigrants' tendency to join communities already established in central and west-central Toronto, and the continuing absence of employment in or around the Beaches. But setting aside the reasons for it, this near absence of European immigrants and the continuing preponderance of Anglos in the population clearly remained a key element of the neighbourhood's social character through the 1950s and 1960s.

Occupational records reveal a similar lack of change. And with no obvious indication that the wages of the neighbourhood's machinists, carpet layers, pressmen, and other tradespeople were much different in the 1960s from what they had been in the 1940s, the socio-economic status of the neighbourhood's population seems to have endured through the early postwar decades. These records also suggest that the neighbourhood's modest residential segregation by class persisted, with the predominantly blue-collar streets of 1941 remaining the predominantly blue-collar streets of 1961.[31]

So too do they show that poverty remained a small but not insignificant part of the neighbourhood's social mix, with casual, low-paid jobs appearing among the thousands of permanent, better-paid occupations. Perhaps even more telling in this regard is that in 1961 18.6 per cent of neighbourhood households had lodgers and 9.6 per cent were home to two full families.[32] Whether this had been the case all along one cannot definitively say, as censuses for the earlier period did not report such details; city directories from early in the century do show some households having more than one adult resident, but it is hard to know how to interpret this. What one can confidently infer from all this, however, is that not everyone in the neighbourhood in 1961 was middle-class affluent. Living standards would improve significantly through the 1960s, with the figures for households with lodgers falling to 10.8 per cent and those with two families to 2.6 per cent by 1971, but evidently not until then were the hardships spawned by a generation of depression and war finally allayed. The persistence of urban poverty in the famously prosperous postwar decades is often overlooked, but here is evidence of it.[33]

But notwithstanding all this continuity, occupation and home ownership records suggest that a modest decline in socio-economic status had occurred in some parts of the neighbourhood between 1941 and 1961.[34] Respectable occupations remained the norm and high-income occupations were not uncommon, but by 1961 some of the better streets seem to have been losing their exclusivity, as the changing ratios of high- to low-status occupations on both Pine Crescent and Neville Park Boulevard reveal.[35] And in 1961 six of the thirty-one substantial houses on Neville Park were occupied by adult non-owners – renters presumably – with blue-collar occupations, a notable change from when the street was built up in the 1920s. These were uncertain years everywhere in old Toronto, with so much of the new population and public investment going into the new suburbs. On top of this, increasing pollution of the lake, and a growing awareness of it, had likely reduced the neighbourhood's recreational appeal to near zero, and might well have lessened the value of its housing, especially near the lake.[36] The Balmy Beach Club, after its clubhouse suffered another damaging fire in the 1960s, considered rebuilding in what its historian has called a "lavish" style but instead opted to build the utilitarian structure – not much different from what it replaced – that occupies the site today.[37] In 1944 A.E. Ames's widow Mary finally sold what remained of the family estate to a developer who subdivided it into over 140 residential lots, and on them, over the next ten years, builders erected houses well below the standard of design in the original Stewart Manor, obviously not targeting the same class of buyers. The manor house itself was reconfigured into seven rental suites.[38]

Mixed in with the neighbourhood's diminishing appeal to those of means is the fact that some of its housing was nearing the end of its natural life by the 1960s. This was especially so along the earliest built-up streets in the west end, where inexpensive wooden housing had been erected on sometimes questionable foundations, but it was apparent in some of the older housing in the former Balmy Beach subdivision too. This early housing was nearly eighty years old. A city-wide housing inventory carried out in 1944 had classed housing in the western part of the neighbourhood, even then, as "declining" and that north of Queen Street in the Balmy Beach area as "vulnerable" to decline (figure 33).[39] It had urged the City to consider renewal of such areas, but the City, having little capacity or budget to do anything, did nothing. By the 1960s, a few owners had demolished older structures and put up new, usually rather inelegant, houses or small apartment buildings in their place, but this was no large-scale solution. The problem of aging housing was not solving itself.

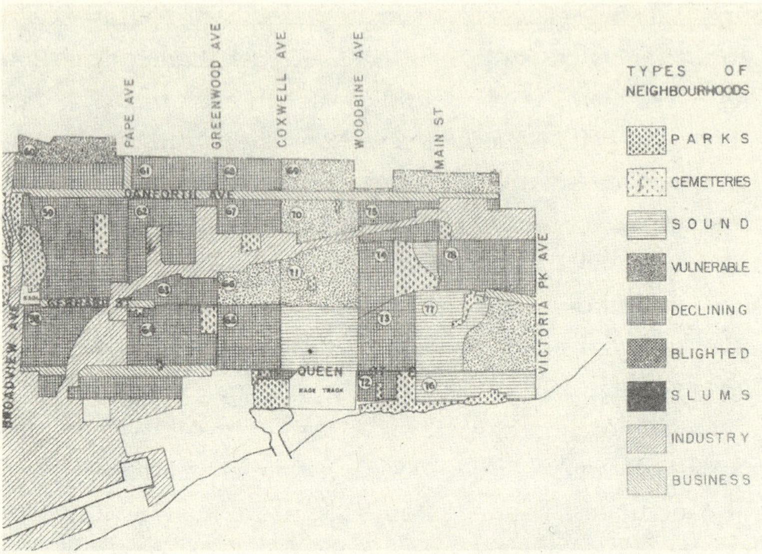

Figure 33. Detail from "Neighbourhood Classifications," *Third Annual Report of the City Planning Board*, Toronto, 31 December 1944. This analysis classes most of old Balmy Beach as "vulnerable" and of old Kew Beach as "declining." Photographs from the time – precious few though they are – suggest this was a fairly accurate assessment.

This decline should not be overdrawn. The neighbourhood population held steady through these postwar decades.[40] Thousands of houses retained their physical integrity and affluent owner-occupants, especially the better-quality brick houses built after 1910.[41] It was mostly the older, wooden houses that had fallen into disrepair – and even some of them remained sound. And while the fact that several large houses on Neville Park Boulevard were being rented does suggest a decline of sorts, these houses offered perfectly good homes to the tenants who rented them. Moreover, twenty-five houses on the street were still owner-occupied, and their depressed values seem to have permitted less wealthy but still respectable middle-class people to own them. Among the owners of these twenty-five houses were a diemaker, a fireman, a schoolteacher, and a young architect, and it is hard to see the presence of such occupations – even on a formerly exclusive street – as an indicator of decline.[42]

Yet there can be no doubt that some of the neighbourhood's housing needed upgrading and that little was being done. And the chief reason for this is surely that so many neighbourhood homeowners lacked the means to do so. Homeowners were not all wealthy. A substantial proportion of the neighbourhood's homes were owned by tradesmen, salesmen, and clerks, not to mention the widows whose deceased husbands had worked in these occupations, and such owners would have lived on modest incomes.[43] Willow Avenue in 1961 is especially striking. Nearly every one of the ninety-eight dwellings in the segment for which ownership was recorded was owned and lived in by a person with a blue-collar occupation.[44] This prevalence of low-income home ownership is noteworthy on its own, but the point here is that it likely deterred substantial renovations. With commercial loans for home renovations nearly impossible to obtain, a renovator had to pay cash, something low-income owners would not have wanted, or been able, to do.[45]

This applied not just to owners of small, low-value homes. Substantial houses initially owned by affluent men often ended up, when these men died, in the hands of their widows or other heirs who lacked the income needed for major upgrades – incomes are not heritable assets – and such owners faced a predicament not unlike that of the owners of low-value houses. Their asset was greater, but the cost of upgrading correspondingly higher. Concern over property values also likely discouraged upgrades, for sensible homeowners do not sink savings into houses of declining value. And one suspects that some owners of older, wooden-frame housing, if they had the means, thought that buying a newer, better-made house in one of the new suburbs made more sense than renovating an aging home in an old congested neighbourhood.[46] Some owners who did not, or could not, sell, and whose house was their only asset, responded by reconfiguring their houses into revenue-producing rental flats, a common strategy among income-poor homeowners in the neighbourhood since the 1920s. But alterations of this type, sometimes done a little crudely, and probably cheaply, did not usually improve the structure or change the appearance of the house.

Whatever the cause of this reluctance to renovate, among its consequences was that the neighbourhood's physical character was preserved. One cannot call this "historical preservation." There is no sign of a preservationist mindset among homeowners; nor did preservationist policies constrain the owners' actions, for there were no such policies. It was simply a matter of homeowners choosing not to alter their homes. But if lack of cash and uncertain property values largely explain this unprescribed preservation by low-income homeowners, something else must have been deterring better-off owners from altering or somehow updating their homes, and infill builders from building in a non-traditional style, for block upon block of neighbourhood streetscapes remained as they had been for decades, free of eye-catching colours or distinctive design. Surely aesthetic conservatism among buyers and owners contributed to this – yet another enduring element of neighbourhood character.

***

Things began to change in the late 1960s, partly owing to the influence of the decade's well-known counterculture movement. Like other parts of the old city in these years the Beaches gained appeal as an "anti-suburb" and began attracting the hippies and yuppies we now know to have been the advance guard of gentrification.[47] And gradually, through the 1970s into the 1980s, the neighbourhood population changed from families of carpenters, clerks, and travelling salesmen to, as Robert Fulford put it, "directors of television commercials, assistant professors of marketing, disc jockeys, and the like."[48] Fulford's characterization seems a little dated now – he was writing in the 1990s, when he was in his sixties – but he was quite right in observing that soft-handed, well-paid workers in the "creative industries" were supplanting the working people he had grown up among. The Beaches was becoming home to a more educated, more affluent population.[49]

The impact of these new arrivals on the neighbourhood's "anthropological landscape" would have been hard to miss. They nearly all had cars – some households had two – which owners began parking on their small front yards. Most could maintain their houses without income from basement suites and attic flats, so they converted houses back to single households, removing rental units. This, together with new arrivals' habit of having smaller families reduced neighbourhood population,[50] resulting in, among other things, lower school enrolment and church attendance, although rampant secularization was mostly responsible for the latter. Rising incomes and women's increasing participation in the paid workforce brought more restaurants to the neighbourhood – only to Queen Street since commerce on residential streets was now formally prohibited. One such restaurant, the Chalet Steakhouse at Queen and Beech, acquired the neighbourhood's first liquor licence in 1975, introducing the already widely adopted – elsewhere, that is – habit of public drinking.[51] Research done some years ago in American urban neighbourhoods found that greater affluence meant less local shopping, and one suspects that happened here too.[52] Perhaps most important for the physical neighbourhood, these new arrivals initiated what ultimately became a comprehensive upgrading of the housing as, one by one, they renovated their homes. Neighbourhood housing was renewed after all, just as the 1944 report had said should be done, although through investments by individual homeowners rather than by public authorities – an outcome the housing analysts in 1944 could not have imagined.

Yet through it all, quite remarkably, the neighbourhood's physical landscape remained mostly intact. Private, house-by-house renewal brought no large-scale redevelopment, no street reconfigurations, no "superblocks," and of course no public housing – in fact none was ever proposed.[53] There was a short-lived threat in the mid-1960s from private developers wanting to build new high-rise apartment buildings, but this was thwarted in one case apparently by local opposition and in another by city planners who concluded the neighbourhood's transportation infrastructure was not up to the demands of a high-rise population and convinced council to reject the development application.[54] No high-rises were ever built. As for the private renovations, notwithstanding countless foundation underpinnings, rear additions, interior wall removals, large new windows, replumbing, rewiring, stylish landscaping, and cedar deck constructions – reflecting the fashions and affluence of the new owners – the residential streetscapes largely retained their appearance. The private upgrading did tend to iron out the spatial differentiation by social class that had marked the original neighbourhood. Houses previously owned by welders and compositors became home to financial advisers and software developers, making streets such as Waverley Road and Willow Avenue more akin to Balsam Avenue, for example, than they had ever been. But most of the incoming residents, different from their predecessors in so many ways, turned out to be as aesthetically conservative as the residents they supplanted.

Opposition to stylistic change had by this time found its way into formal policies. Beginning in 1969, Toronto's Official Plan required that, in the words of the current plan, "development in established neighbourhoods ... respect and reinforce the existing physical character" of the neighbourhood it is in,[55] and as of 1974 the Ontario Heritage Act empowered municipalities to designate certain areas as Heritage Conservation Districts in which building renovation and alteration were strictly controlled.[56] But these policies were not the cause of the neighbourhood's preservation; streets remained as they were because of choices made by owners and builders – the latter reflecting the preferences of buyers, as always – not because of government policy.

Figure 34. East side of Leuty Avenue, c. 1972. A moment of everyday life that could as easily be 1942 or 2002 as 1972. The neighbourhood endures.

Courtesy of Toronto Public Library (LOCHIST-BE-017)

To date only one street in the neighbourhood, Kingswood Road South, has been designated a Heritage Conservation District, yet dozens of the neighbourhood's streets still look much as they did a century ago (figure 34).[57]

So we come to the twenty-first century, to a neighbourhood often described as having the look and feel of an old Ontario town, which in some ways it does. It was never a town unto itself of course, having always been an appendage of Toronto, but with so much of its original character still intact it does seem to have not yet entered the twenty-first century. Its high proportion of ethnic British and low proportion of "visible minorities" persists, as does its social range from lower-middle- to upper-middle-class, with little of the real poverty and extreme wealth evident elsewhere in contemporary Toronto.[58] It has countless restaurants, but none of the chic, highbrow variety found in more affluent city neighbourhoods. Most of its houses remain those built by the competent if unschooled builders of the early twentieth century, and these houses still tightly line its rectilinear grid of streets and still show barely a hint of modern design. The ongoing replacement of older, smaller houses marches on, gradually but only slightly changing the look of some streetscapes; watered-down modern, or perhaps one might say postmodern, designs have begun to appear, but they remain rare, and despite being far from avant-garde still draw headshakes and tut-tuts from passersby.[59] Its century-old low-rise apartment buildings still stand amid the residential fabric (an element of physical character that current policies protect but would never permit). The neighbourhood remains purely residential, with no employment to speak of, and its commerce remains confined to its still strikingly small-town main street. It continues to be served by streetcar, and still resembles a streetcar suburb even though, in truth, it is not one – current residents being wealthy enough, current streetcars slow and unreliable enough, and current employment dispersed enough that most residents drive cars to their jobs. But all told, notwithstanding numerous changes in its "anthropological landscape," its overall character, a product of actions taken over a century ago, endures.

One important element of the neighbourhood that has changed over the near-century of its existence is the waterfront park – the exception that proves the rule in a sense, for, as discussed at length, the park ceased belonging to the neighbourhood in the 1930s and has been free to evolve a character of its own. Walking through the park today, along the boardwalk, through the grassy picnic areas, or on the beach itself, one hears plenty of languages other than English. The proportion of Anglo residents remains high among neighbourhood residents, but not in the park, whose daily users reflect present-day Toronto in a way the residential neighbourhood does not. Yet accompanying this has been an important change in attitude. Local residents rarely picnic beside or swim in the lake – they dine on their decks and drive to their cottages – but they do stroll the boardwalk. Yet never will one hear complaints about outsiders using the park. Unusual architecture still elicits disapproval; large gatherings of non-Anglo picnickers no longer do. Some things change, even in the Beaches.

CHAPTER EIGHT

Conclusion: History in the Contemporary Landscape

Over the last two generations some insightful urban geographers and landscape historians have advanced the notion that urban landscapes can serve as windows to the past, that even something as mundane as a common streetscape reveals something about who or what created it and how or when it was created.[1] Espousing this notion transforms one's perception of urban environments. City streets become material history exhibits that convey not just the design ideas or economic conditions that prevailed at the time of their creation – although they do that – but also, in some cases, what its creators thought and how they operated. It is with such ideas in mind that this book concludes by exploring the neighbourhood's present-day landscapes in search of its history, with the objective, at least in part, of finding evidence of what this book has recounted in the streets, parks, and houses of today.[2] An important complement to this quest, of course, is to find aspects of the neighbourhood's past that the present-day landscapes do *not* reveal.

***

The absence of planning, though perhaps not visible in a single, static sighting, is hard to miss after a few blocks. The first sign might be the north-south streets not lining up as they cross the main central thoroughfare, Queen Street; even where a street *name* crosses Queen the street itself often jogs. What one is seeing here is the neighbourhood's subdivision process, in which blocks of privately owned land were subdivided independently, according to the wishes of their owners, with no overall plan or public authority shaping or controlling the layouts. A few streets do line up, but only in cases where subdivision was done at the very start of the development process, by owners who held land on both sides of Queen Street; Lee and Beech Avenues are the most significant examples of this.

Queen Street itself also offers evidence of non-planning. First is its standard sixty-six-foot width, chosen with complete disregard for its function as a *rue principale*; this is particularly striking now, with enormous new streetcars barrelling (traffic permitting) along the street – their scale quite ill-suited to streets not planned for this function. Second is the street's unusual mix of commercial and residential land uses together with the curious grafting of commercial extensions on the fronts of its residential buildings, both of which reflect the lack of land-use planning at the time of the street's build-up. This absence may be less problematic than the street's width today, and no doubt it appeals to those who favour the principle of mixed-use or who enjoy the neighbourhood's small-town look. Present-day shop owners might think otherwise, wishing the street was better suited to loading and unloading, which it would be if it had it been dedicated to commercial use from the start, or at least somehow converted to that use in the 1920s once its commercial function was established. But benefits or disbenefits aside, the street is a vivid artifact of the neighbourhood's unplanned past.

One also sees the absence of planning in the lack of public squares and other designated open spaces. There is no lack of open space overall, for the neighbourhood is well served by its three large public parks; the lack of open space is within the residential fabric, and here again is the absence of a comprehensive neighbourhood plan, or of any public authority placing demands on private subdividers. Most of the dozen or so plans of subdivision that gave the neighbourhood its basic structure set aside no land for public space. Why would private landowners give away residential lots they could sell? Whether the neighbourhood suffers from this is another matter. Jane Jacobs ridiculed neighbourhood parks in her 1961 book *Death and Life of Great American Cities* – describing them as "dispirited city vacuums called parks" – and some planners still side with her. But the absence of such spaces, shortcoming or not, is another revealing historical artifact.[3]

Two cases might be considered exceptions to this absence of park planning. One is Balmy Beach Park, part of a plan in a sense, for Wilson's 1876 plan of subdivision did designate this land as open space. But one can go only so far with this because the park today is not what Wilson's plan proposed. We do not actually know what it proposed, for the Balmy Beach "plan" included no landscape design whatsoever, weakening the claim of the park being planned. We do know Wilson envisioned it as a private park, not a public park – and in doing so was quite out of step with the park planning movement that emerged in his later years – and he certainly did not envision a large clubhouse and extensive parking lot amid his "private promenade." Present-day Balmy Beach Park provides evidence of its curious quasi-exclusive origins and of the City's unwillingness to challenge the "founder" status of Balmy Beach Club, but not of park planning. The other case is Glen Stewart Park. Provident Investments always knew this property was potential parkland – indeed G.A. Cox had once considered making the entire estate into a park. It also knew it could not build safely on the bottomlands and that by keeping the whole central corridor in a natural state it was enhancing the value of every lot it sold. So the park might be considered planned, or at least envisioned, in a general sense, but by a corporate landowner in its own interest as part of a single residential precinct, not by a public authority as part of the neighbourhood overall. These two parks were and still are fine additions to the neighbourhood, but they show the absence of true park planning more than its presence.

The entire residential fabric was unplanned, of course, and this also is hard to miss. The rectilinear grid pays no heed to topography, streets sometimes dead-end at property lines, roadways are of inconsistent width, tracts of multiple hillside lots are sometimes levelled in defiance of the grade (necessitating some imposing retaining walls at the downhill end of the levelled tracts), houses on some streets are oddly placed on their lots, and apartments and rowhouses crop up in random locations. Whether this matters is, once again, an open question. The streets could perhaps be more efficiently laid out, but the narrow streets, the extreme density, the hodgepodge of housing types, and the irregular setbacks are hardly a problem, and in fact lend a rather appealing, pre-modern charm, while a few well-liked features of the neighbourhood, such as the absence of industry or the permeable social boundaries, happened anyway, without planning. Planning, evidently, was not necessary to create a functional neighbourhood – in the early twentieth century at least – for what one sees in the physical and social fabric of the Beaches, like it or not, is the product of non-planning.

Looking closely at the housing, at least that built before 1914, one can read nearly the entire process of its creation: practical builders, working in an open market, with potential buyers neither sophisticated nor affluent, building individual family dwellings in a conventional, functional style, taking design cues from their rural/small-town backgrounds and from what they saw being built and sold around them.[4] That is to say the neighbourhood's housing, like the neighbourhood's structure, reflects the values, skills, and strategies of individual entrepreneurs working under the invisible hand of the market. And taking a wider view, the streetscapes reveal something of the building process too, the many groups of two, three, or four nearly identical houses showing the multiplicity of builders involved in the neighbourhood's creation.

The one exception to this absence of professional planning and design is the Stewart Manor district (now generally known as Glen Manor). It stands out in several ways. First in its topography, for its valley sides, especially where they meet the main escarpment, create a rolling landscape unlike that anywhere else in the neighbourhood. But also in its professionally designed layout, which when contrasted with the unplanned northward extension of Kenilworth Avenue into comparable terrain, shows the impact of comprehensive top-down planning, unfragmented land ownership, and skilled landscape designers. The district's housing, nearly all of it architect-designed, stands out too, reflecting the building restrictions imposed by the property developer, Provident Investments.

The enclave is also distinct in having within it the oldest house in the neighbourhood – the Ames House, the core of which is the Darling House, built on the brow of the ravine in 1873. The house was purchased in 1900 and subsequently expanded by A.E. Ames, who occupied it until his death in 1934. His wife Mary (sometimes referred to as Minnie) remained until 1944, when she sold it and its surrounding property for residential development. The house appears essentially as it was after its 1947 conversion into rental suites; in fact, judging from old photographs its exterior is not much changed from Ames's day, notwithstanding its front door now being on what was originally the back of the house.[5] The outlook down the ravine – one can only imagine this since its back (formerly front) yard is private property – might be the closest we can get to a pre-suburb vista. But this erstwhile estate has something more to tell us. That the old house still stands, consisting of non-luxury rental units, and that the land below the house on Long Crescent and beside it on Lee Avenue is built up with modest, rather commonplace housing – all this the product of the 1940s and 1950s – offers vivid evidence of the enclave's lost exclusivity in the immediate postwar years.

***

Although a suburb, the Beaches was built before earth-moving machinery had the capacity it has today; indeed, the symbolic creator of modern suburbia, the bulldozer, had not yet been invented when the Beaches was built.[6] So the natural landscape of the neighbourhood was not as altered by its construction as one might think. Several natural features survive. Most noticeable might be the original contours of the land. Travelling the length of the neighbourhood along Queen Street one rises and falls ever so slightly as one traverses the terrain's original, now-filled, hills and vales, the deepest and most noticeable of the latter being at Ivan Forrest Gardens, where the street crosses what was once a wetland fed by the stream flowing down Darling's/Ames's wooded ravine.[7] The City had to fill this "gully," as the locals apparently called it,[8] before the street railway would extend its tracks to the city limit at Maclean Avenue. The City did so in 1893, making the street dry and stable enough for streetcars though still, clearly, well short of level. The fill created, or perhaps allowed the Howard family to create, the substantial spring-fed pond north of the street (see figure 12). The pond is long gone – drained in the 1930s – but its contours, and the spring that fed it, remain.[9]

Other places offer further evidence of diverted streams or drained wetlands. One is along Kenilworth Avenue, north of Queen Street, where signs of a small, vanished floodplain are hard to miss in the low flat terrain and old weeping willow trees, whose preference for stream beds is well known. But present-day housing shows the lost wetland too. A 1903 plan of subdivision had extended Kenilworth north of Queen, but the only lots built up at that time were on the high ground above the west side of the street, where a stretch of mostly brick houses stands to this day.[10] On the east side, and along the road extending north into the wetland – called for a time Kenilworth Crescent – very little building occurred, and in fact records and photographs show that until well into the 1920s those lots had only low-value wooden houses, some of them rural enough to have likely predated the 1903 subdivision.[11] It was not until after the land was drained in the 1920s and 1930s – part of a complex draining and filling by the City – that owners of these lots built permanent structures, including apartment buildings where lots were large enough, making this lower part of Kenilworth, with a few exceptions, a generation newer than the upper. This temporal difference tells us that registering a plan of subdivision, even in the pre-1914 building boom, was not enough to make swampland valuable, and reminds anyone who needs reminding that the neighbourhood's builders were not fools.

Another former watercourse is visible where Willow Avenue meets the lake. Willow Avenue was not a street in the original Balmy Beach subdivision. It was simply the line where the villa-size lots fronting on Birch and Beech

Avenues met, and south of Queen Street this line, being the lowest land in the vicinity, was the location of a small stream that drained the area (see figure 5). Willow Avenue north of Queen Street was carved out of the villa lots and built up before 1914, but south of Queen no street was created because of the stream. The stream is gone now, its flow having been diverted in the 1920s into underground conduits, allowing its streambed to be filled and Willow Avenue to be paved and built-up – its houses noticeably newer than houses north of Queen, and more akin to those in the contemporaneous amusement park redevelopment.[12] But the stream's course, which veered east at the foot of Willow Avenue, can still be imagined where the land – now a playground – slopes down to what was the stream's original embouchement at the foot of Silver Birch. One will also sometimes see evidence of the wetland that once covered the southern parts of Williams's Kew Gardens property. It was fed by streams flowing in from the northeast, signs of which remain in the current park's topography. But more vivid evidence appears whenever a high water table turns the southern portion of Kew Gardens into pools of standing water, revealing how little landfill the Parks Department brought in after the City acquired the property in 1907.[13]

The beach might be considered another enduring natural feature, though in fact it is almost as much a product of human agency as the streets and houses. Owners and users of waterfront land preferred sandy beach to reedy wetland – the natural condition of much of the shore – so over the years the City did what it could to expand and enhance the beach at the expense of the natural ecosystem. Scientists have calculated that some 90 per cent of Toronto's lakefront wetlands have been have lost to landfilling over the two centuries of the city's existence, and the Beaches neighbourhood has received its share of that fill.[14] The beach has also been altered by underground sewers, the flow of which one often hears beneath the manhole covers. The sound of water at the beach is not always natural.

The lake, of course, is an enduring natural feature. Notwithstanding the occasional sewer outfall or beach-enhancing groyne – the latter all now buried under the sand they were built to entrap – the lake remains a powerful presence, moderating temperatures, reflecting the sky, and offering the thrill of crashing surf on stormy days. Proximity to the lake was the reason Toronto people first came to the district, and although one cannot say it is why the residential neighbourhood was created – new housing was built almost anywhere in Toronto in the early 1900s – the lake remained a fact of neighbourhood life throughout the twentieth century. Pollution lessened its appeal in the 1960s and 1970s, but what was lost has been mostly regained, and the lake now is as attractive as ever. Few people swim in it, for various reasons, but countless visitors enjoy it from the shore, walking alongside it and gazing out at it year-round. The lake, maybe more than the beach, is the strongest natural continuity in the Beaches' history.[15]

Since the area was not extensively farmed neither was it extensively cleared of forest and bush by its earliest owners; widespread clearing occurred later, when the housing was built. Photographs from the tower of the newly completed (1906) Kew Beach firehall show patches of natural woods – bush really – still standing between clusters of the new wooden-clad houses.[16] These photographs also show trees, both evergreen and deciduous, lining some residential streets, their placement suggesting they had been planted after the streets were made. But given their 1906 size they are more likely "residual trees"[17] – naturally germinated trees left in place when the houses were built, something that was possible when excavation was done by pick and shovel. Many such trees still exist, most of them oaks, now over a century old, identifiable by their sometimes illogical, probably unchosen, locations overly close to laneways and houses.

Along the untended edges of some back lanes or the yards of long-neglected houses one sometimes sees other plants that might have survived land-clearing and housebuilding, some perhaps having started life alongside a cultivated farm field. Wild grape vines, known to be long-lived plants, are a good bet for this. One nearly ubiquitous wild plant is the orange daylily (*Hemerocallis fulva*). It is not native. Garden historians tell us it was brought to the Atlantic colonies by the earliest English settlers and that it spread throughout the Great Lakes region as settlement moved west. It likely arrived in the Beaches with the first landowners or early tenant farmers. It turned out to be ineradicable, and flourishes today in patches both tended and wild, an integral element of the neighbourhood's early summer landscape. Since it reproduces by spawning new tubers, the daylilies we see today are likely clones of those brought in at the start of settlement, meaning that, genetically speaking, they have been here longer than the parks and private gardens they adorn – they too, like the towering red and white oaks, artifacts of the pre-suburb past.

***

What can the present-day landscape tell us about the people who created the neighbourhood? One revealing detail is that the largest original buildings are the churches, five of them, now all so tightly surrounded by other structures they are easy to overlook. They represent the main Protestant Christian sects: (from west to east) Baptist, Methodist, Presbyterian – these latter two became the United Church in 1924 – independent Presbyterian (after 1924), and Anglican. These substantial buildings were erected at considerable expense, with donations and volunteer effort from their parishioners – most of these churches had memberships of more than a thousand up to the 1950s, when the decline in mainstream Christianity began.[18] The Beaches evidently was created by church-going people. There is also a synagogue, a building that began life in the 1890s as a small Baptist church, whose congregation grew so large in a single generation that it needed a new, correspondingly large church, which it built two blocks away (Waverley Road Baptist).[19] A few dozen local Jewish families bought the disused church in 1919 and converted it into their own place of worship, later reworking the front facade into a more suitable style. The central importance of organized worship in the early twentieth century is easy for those in a more secular age to forget, but it is hard to miss in the urban landscape.[20]

The presence of the synagogue should not be taken to convey religious diversity in the neighbourhood's early population. The Jews who established the synagogue were few. They were for the most part well-established, English-speaking Canadians, a generation or more past immigration, who, one community member remembers, "led productive and satisfying lives and got along well with their non-Jewish neighbours."[21] So the synagogue does remind us that, notwithstanding the disturbances of August 1933, Jews were generally accepted in the Beaches.[22] But demographically they were scarcely measurable. Moreover, one will see that the neighbourhood still includes not a single Roman Catholic church (one just west and one just north of the neighbourhood were built in the 1920s).[23] The urban landscape reminds us that the Beaches at the time of its creation was not just overwhelmingly Christian. It was overwhelmingly Protestant Christian.

We also see how important education was to the founding residents, for three substantial public schools were built in the early years. Kew Beach was the first, Balmy Beach the second (built by the East Toronto school board), and Williamson Road the third (built on land purchased from National Trust [formerly owned by Ames] after the 1909 annexation).[24] Schools with those names still stand on their original sites, though the two older have been replaced by modern structures that look less like traditional urban schoolhouses. These schools might be even less noticeable than the churches in the present-day landscape, but they are as telling. The priority given to building them, with funds contributed by all city ratepayers – including those without children – reveals a deeply held collective commitment to public education in the city at large as well as in the neighbourhood. The presence of three schools in a single neighbourhood also reminds us of the large number of children in the neighbourhood's houses; enrolments at these early schools are difficult, if not impossible, to ascertain, but with average Canadian household size more than double what it is today, and fertility rates roughly triple, a school recess in 1910 would have been heard blocks away.[25]

Though poverty was present, the Beaches was by no means poor. The tradesmen, small business owners, and mid-level white-collar workers who bought and occupied the first houses – as discussed at length – were basically the emerging middle class of Edwardian urban society, and many either were or were on the way to becoming property owners. But the small lots and modest housing of the neighbourhood convey the message that its original inhabitants, for whom or by whom these houses were built, were frugal, or at least disinclined to indulge. Even the better houses of Stewart Manor show little sign of "conspicuous consumption," the term coined by American sociologist Thorstein Veblen around the time the neighbourhood's first houses were being built.[26] Veblen would not have coined it living in Toronto's Beaches.

***

Next to nothing of the neighbourhood's cottage era remains in the current landscape. Nearly all lakefront structures were demolished and cleared away by the City, first in 1907–8 to create Kew Gardens and then in 1931 to create Eastern Beaches Waterfront Park. Some of the small houses at the bottom of Leuty Avenue, their cores at least, may have been built in Justus Dunn's subdivision in the 1880s, for cottages on Leuty extended far enough up from the beach to escape the comprehensive 1931 demolition, but most of the small wooden frame houses still standing elsewhere in the Kew Beach residential area, though some look like cottages, were inexpensive year-round homes.[27]

Balmy Beach is somewhat different. The City demolished all the lakefront structures there too, including the few large summer homes dating from the community's founding years. But in Balmy Beach, unlike Kew Beach, some substantial cottage-style homes were built well away from the lake, and these were untouched by lakefront expropriations. Most of these, despite their rustic details, were year-round residences, although some were used seasonally at first by those who could afford to maintain two homes.[28] But even if they were year-round homes, their designs were cottage-inspired and thus they reflect Balmy Beach's origins as a recreational community. One can see them today, scattered throughout the residential fabric, distinguishable by their clapboard and/or shingle exteriors and their open porches. One vestige of a commercial hotel even remains – the row of family rental units built as Pine Terrace shortly after 1900 on the east side of Beech Avenue above Queen Street, now an unusual run of privately owned row houses aligned perpendicular to the street. So although Balmy Beach's lakefront cottages were removed, its residential landscape holds reminders of its recreational past – though one must look hard to find them.

The cottage years are not the only major piece of neighbourhood history of which the present-day landscape offers no evidence. Returning to the starting point of this history, another is the long period of Indigenous presence on the land. Oddly, somebody who did mention it was Bert Ganter, one of the two young men behind the Swastika disturbances of 1933. On being pressed by a reporter to explain why, if his group truly was not antisemitic, they were using the swastika symbol, "Ganter replied that the Balmy Beach area had at one time been a camping ground for the Iroquois Indians, to whom the Swastika used to be a sign of good luck."[29] His statement is curious but plausible, regarding both the camping ground and the Swastika. One cannot know whether Ganter was informed or simply making something up to deflect the question. Be that as it may, while this exchange is not representative of anything, it suggests that the neighbourhood's Indigenous past, though absent from the landscape then and now, was not entirely absent from everyday thinking. One day we may know more about it.

There is also scant evidence of agriculture in the present-day landscape, and unlike the cottages, which we know existed and were removed, we know so little about past agriculture that we do not even know what evidence, if any, has been lost (although we can be sure some was cleared away in the construction of Scarboro Beach Amusement Park). But it is hard to believe, notwithstanding the paucity of evidence, that in the century between land granting and suburb building nobody in this settler society farmed the land. And we do have fragments of documentary evidence, from the second half of the nineteenth century at least.[30] As recounted in earlier chapters: Joseph Williams bought a farm in the 1850s and immediately began selling produce from it, farmers cultivated what became Thomas O'Connor's land (later Provident Farm) prior to the 1850s, Justus Dunn was a land-owning market gardener in the 1880s, a William Stinson cultivated a market garden on one of Allan Maclean Howard's lots in 1891, a market gardener named William Seal occupied James Lumbers's large cottage lot in 1897–8, a local farmer sold milk from a cart along Balmy Beach streets about 1900,[31] and as late as 1914 the owner of a lot on Leuty Avenue identified himself as a farmer (but we do not know if he farmed it). These fragments tell us that farming was being done on patches of suitable, available land when permanent residents began arriving in the late nineteenth century – likely furnishing the early residents with produce – but they tell us little about farming in the first half-century of settler ownership. In any case, these details are from documentary sources. The present-day urban landscape tells us nothing whatsoever.

Another missing piece of the historical tableau is the period of modest decline from the 1930s through to the 1960s. Few photographs from these years are to be found in public repositories. The neighbourhood seems to have been unloved by residents and little-admired by visitors, and neither old nor new enough to draw much attention. Nor was it in such an advanced state of dereliction that it was inventoried in preparation for full-on urban renewal, as some old inner-city neighbourhoods were. The City Architect's Department did photograph a few truly dilapidated structures, but such buildings were rare and unrepresentative.[32] The visual record, all told, offers little. The present-day landscape is equally unforthcoming. The few inelegant duplexes and low-rise apartment buildings from the 1950s and 1960s are evidence of a sort, suggesting a derelict wooden structure once stood on their site. But that is all the landscape reveals. With nearly every aging, neglected house having been either rebuilt and enhanced or demolished and replaced, the neighbourhood's generation of decline is as invisible as its cottaging and farming.

Appendix

Beaches Neighbourhood Residents, 1900–1961

The research presented here was undertaken to gain insight into two important but unexplored aspects of the neighbourhood's early history – its social makeup and the employment locations of its employed residents. It had been done by a historian with limited experience in quantitative historical research, as any historian with more experience will immediately observe. As such, its methodology undoubtedly falls short of the standards of true quantitative analysis – data selection has not been random; data counts and calculations have been done manually (with pencil and calculator), and are thus subject to error; and the compilation and interpretation have not been subjected to any rigorous outside review. But as humanist historians have asserted more than once in defence of such work, while certainly not the final word on the matter even these more casual compilations surely say something.

The data were drawn from Toronto City Directories, large reference volumes produced and sold annually by Might Directories Limited from 1875 (other commercial firms produced similar volumes prior to this) through to the mid-twentieth century. They were not official public documents – unlike municipal assessment rolls, which recorded similar information – but they are considered accurate, based as they were on door-to-door canvassing. Researchers have relied on them for years.

These directories are invaluable here for two reasons. One is that they have been digitized and put online by the Internet Archive and are readily available through the website of the Toronto Public Library.[1] Since the later stages of research for this book were done during the pandemic emergency of the early 2020s, with libraries and archives closed to the public, these online volumes were a lifesaver. (Assessment rolls were not available online.) The other reason is their unique content. In addition to listing city residents alphabetically by name, like any "phone book," these directories list city streets alphabetically by name, with the name of the primary resident (prior to the 1950s, the man of the house if there was one) of every residence, listed sequentially by address number, on each street. Furthermore, and quite remarkably, the alphabetical listing of residents – to which one could turn after identifying the residents of a particular street segment – provides the occupation and usually the employer of most primary residents. Both were essential to this research – occupations provided insight into the social class of residents, and employers (when they and their address were given) provided information on journeys to work.

Data have been compiled for twenty street segments at various years. The size of the segments varies with the nature and length of the street, and as a result the number of residents in each segment ranges widely, from a few dozen to over one hundred. The segments were not selected randomly but were chosen by the author to include the range of housing types and occupations present in the neighbourhood, and in some cases to identify change over time.

Occupations were assigned to one of five categories: blue collar, administrative/clerical, sales, manager/proprietor, and professional. This assignment involved personal judgment, and as such is open to question. Both skilled and unskilled labourers were classed blue-collar, for example, while tradesmen running their own firm (e.g., sheet metal and roofing) were classed manager/proprietor. And the boundary between the administrative/clerical and the manager/proprietor categories was not always easy to set. But the categorization has been done consistently, making comparisons within the sample valid. These five categories were grouped into two status levels – the first three being "low status" and the last two "high status." This is a rather crude dichotomy, admittedly. Classifying a self-employed accountant, who might have a small client base, as higher status than a skilled machinist or electrician with a full-time job might seem off the mark, especially without any information on their incomes. It has been done here in deference to the long-standing convention, warranted or not, that "the professions" carry a degree of social status, together with a belief that the number of residents with this status would have affected the social character of a street.

For the earlier years, the location of employment was also noted, the main objective being to determine whether the neighbourhood was in fact a "streetcar suburb" (it was). This compilation was done for only a few of the post-1920 segments. Employment locations were not as easy to identify for these later years. And with the wider distribution of employment and the likelihood of some travel being done by automobile, especially after 1950, there seemed little value in pursuing this as thoroughly as for the earlier years.

Location of Segments

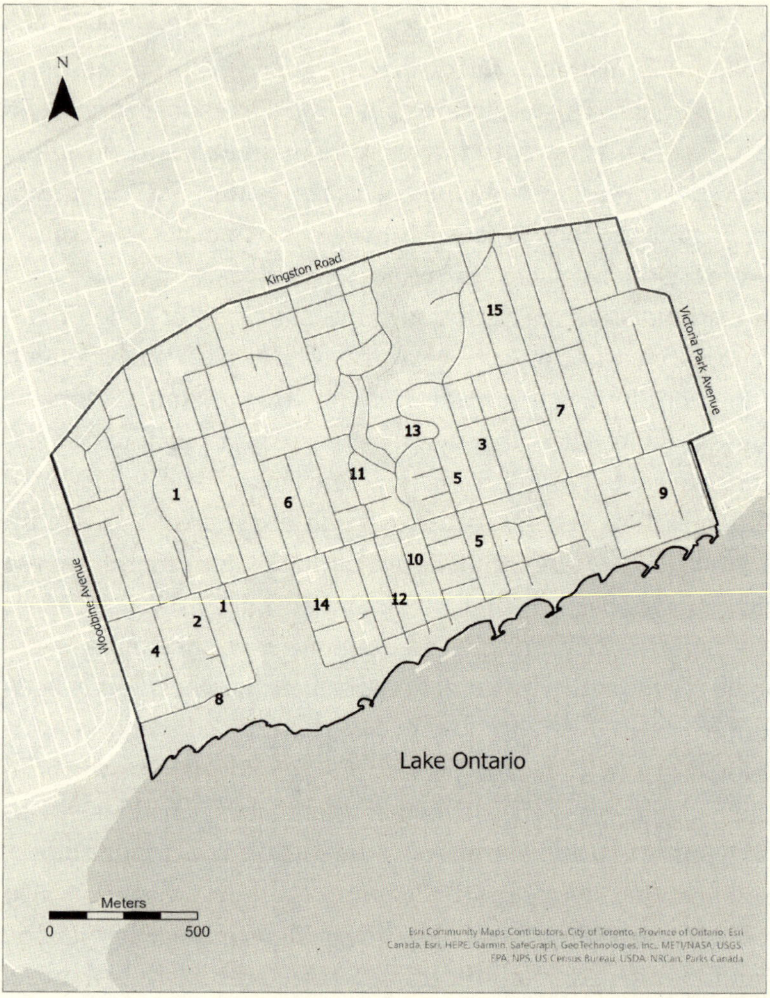

1. **Waverley Road**
   - 1900, 1910: north from lake to city limit just north of Queen Street, both sides
   - 1951: east side, from lake north to Norway Avenue; west side, north to Queen Street

2. **Kenilworth Avenue**, 1905
   - north from lake to city limit just north of Queen Street, both sides

3. **Spruce Hill Road**, 1910
   - north from Queen Street to Pine Avenue, both sides

4. **Kippendavie Avenue**, 1910
   - north from lake to Queen Street, both sides

5. **Balsam Avenue**
   - 1910: north from lake to Pine Avenue, both sides
   - 1951: east side, from lake north to terminus at Willow Avenue; west side, from lake north to Queen Street

6. **Hambly Avenue**, 1912
   - north from Queen Street to Williamson Road, west side only

7. **Silver Birch Avenue**, 1912
   - north from lake to Kingston Road, east side only

8. **Kew Beach**, 1912
   - lakefront lots (not a street) east from Woodbine Avenue to Scarboro Beach Amusement Park

9. **Neville Park Boulevard**, 1924, 1961
   - north from lake to Queen Street, both sides

10. **Glen Manor Road**, 1931
    - north from lake to Queen Street, west side only

11. **Glen Manor Road West**, 1931
    - west side of ravine, north of Queen Street, from Glen Manor Drive to Beaufort Road

12. **Scarborough Beach Boulevard**, 1941 and 1961
    - north from lake to Queen Street, both sides

13. **Pine Crescent**, 1941 and 1961
    - east from Glen Manor Drive, following 'S' curve, to Balsam Avenue, both sides

14. **Leuty Avenue**, 1961
    - north from lake to Queen Street, both sides

15. **Willow Avenue**
    - 1914: north from Queen Street to Balsam Avenue, both sides
    - 1961: north from Pine Avenue to Balsam Avenue, both sides (level portion)

TABLE 1. *Employment Classification: Original Streetcar Suburb (to 1914)*

Classifications:

BC: Blue Collar (skilled trades, unskilled workers, service jobs)

Sales: Sales (jobs identified as such, includes "travellers," lower-level sales supervisors)

A/C: Administrative/Clerical (lower-level white collar)

P/M: Proprietor/Manager (any business owner, includes builders, upper management of large firms)

Prof: Professional (wide range from musician to barrister, independent or employee)

SEGMENT (Street/Year)	Residents Counted	No Job Info	Low Status			High Status		High:Low Status Ratio (in per cent)
			BC	Sales	A/C	P/M	Prof	
Waverley Road 1900	29	3	6	8	5	6	1	27:73
Kenilworth Avenue 1905	18	4	11	1	2	0	0	0:100
Waverley Road 1910	115	18	50	14	16	16	1	18:82
Spruce Hill Road 1910	53	9	12	8	9	12	3	34:66
Kippendavie Avenue 1910	55	10	28	2	11	2	2	9:91
Balsam Avenue 1910	60	9	5	6	9	24	7	61:39
Hambly Avenue 1912	33	3	6	5	12	6	1	23:77
Silver Birch Avenue 1912	40	15	8	4	3	10	0	40:60
Kew Beach 1912	41	10	13	3	2	7	6	42:58
Willow Avenue 1914	87	16	40	6	14	6	5	15:85
TOTALS	531	97	179	57	83	89	26	27:73

TABLE 2. *Employment Classification: Subsequent Evolution (1920 to 1961)*

Classifications:
BC: Blue Collar (skilled trades, unskilled workers, service jobs)
Sales: Sales (jobs identified as such, includes "travellers," lower-level supervisors)
A/C: Administrative/Clerical (lower-level white collar)
P/M: Proprietor/Manager (any business owner, includes builders, upper management of large firms)
Prof: Professional (wide range from musician to barrister, independent or employee)

SEGMENT	Residents Counted	No Job Info	Low Status			High Status		High:Low Status Ratio (in per cent)
			BC	Sales	A/C	P/M	Prof	
Neville Park Blvd 1924	24	2	0	5	1	12	4	73:27
Glen Manor Drive 1931	31	4	6	7	7	2	5	26:74
Glen Manor Drive W 1931	23	2	1	3	5	10	2	57:43
Pine Crescent 1941	61	8 +2 ms*	1	9	3	22	16	75:25
Scarborough Beach Blvd 1941	109	16 +2 ms*	31	9	34	9	8	19:81
Balsam Avenue 1951	199	58	41	23	53	17	7	17:83
Waverly Road 1951	193	52	75	5	50	3	8	8:92
Leuty Avenue 1961	128	35 +1 ms*	54	7	25	2	4	7:93
Scarborough Beach Blvd 1961	112	47	17	7	24	9	8	26:74
Pine Crescent 1961	69	18	4	9	9	13	16	57:43
Neville Park Blvd 1961	37	9	6	3	5	9	5	50:50
Willow Avenue 1961	129	28	65	7	22	1	6	7:93
TOTALS	1115	280	301	94	238	109	89	24:76

* active military service

TABLE 3. *Employment Location: Streetcar Suburb (1900–14)*

SEGMENT (Street/Date)	Employment Known	Employment Location Stated*	Downtown	East of Lower Don River	Beaches
Waverley Road 1900	26	18	18	0	0
Kenilworth Avenue 1905	14	7	5	1	1
Waverley Road 1910	97	60	55	2	3
Spruce Hill Road 1910	44	27	25	1	1
Kippendavie Avenue 1910	45	19	17	0	2
Balsam Avenue 1910	51	43	41	1	1
Hambly Avenue 1912	30	21	20	0	1
Silver Birch Avenue 1912	25	11	9	1	1
Kew Beach 1912	31	18	15	2	1
Willow Avenue 1914	71	37	35	0	2
TOTALS		261	240**	8**	13

* No location stated for many trades, especially construction trades

** Together, 248 locations accessed by streetcar, 95% of known locations

TABLE 4. *Employment Location: Subsequent Evolution (1920–61)*

In this later period, employment locations were not always stated in the sources used, making this measure less meaningful,so employment locations were determined for only some street segments. The findings suggested that downtown remained the primary location of employment, that the Carlaw industrial area had become a significant location for blue-collar work, that employment locations were becoming more disperse, and that local neighbourhood employment remained negligible, but these suggestions were not firm conclusions. And how people travelled to their jobs could not be determined.

SEGMENT (Steet/Date)	Employment Known	Employment Location Stated	Downtown	Other	Beaches
Neville Park Blvd 1924					
Glen Manor Drive 1931	27	19	16	3	0
Glen Manor Drive W 1931					
Pine Crescent 1941	53	47	38	6	3
Scarborough Beach Blvd 1941					
Balsam Avenue 1951					
Waverley Road 1951	141	95	61	31*	3
Leuty Avenue 1961					
Scarborough Beach Blvd 1961	65	57	37	18	2
Pine Crescent 1961					
Neville Park Blvd 1961	28	21	11	5	5
Willow Avenue 1961					

*Of which 25 were east side of lower Don River (as in table 3)

Abbreviations

AR	Assessment Roll
BC	Board of Control
CT	City of Toronto
CTA	City of Toronto Archives
CTCMs	City of Toronto Council Minutes
TCD	Toronto City Directory
Cttee	Committee
DCB	*Dictionary of Canadian Biography*, 15 volumes (Toronto: University of Toronto Press, 1966–)
ET	East Toronto
OLRO	Ontario Land Registry Office
R	Report
RP	Registered Plan of Subdivision
TPL	Toronto Public Library
UBC	University of British Columbia
UT	University of Toronto

Notes

"Goad's Atlases," frequently cited in the following notes, are compilations of detailed city maps prepared intermittently from the mid-nineteenth to the early twentieth centuries by the Charles E. Goad Company for sale to the insurance industry. Digital copies of these atlases are accessible online through various portals. For this research, Toronto atlases were accessed at the privately run oldtorontomaps.blogspot.com. The even more detailed plans, on which maps in the atlases were based, though rare, also exist, and they too are cited on occasion.

Introduction

1 2016 population (21,567) from CT Neighbourhood Profile: www.toronto.ca/ext/sdfa/Neighbourhood%20Profiles/pdf/2016/pdf1/cpa63.pdf; 1941 population (26,393) from "Population and Housing Characteristics by Census Tracts – Toronto," Census of Canada 1951. The two figures apply to identical areas, but that area is not identical to the neighbourhood defined for this study.

2 City of Toronto Neighbourhood Profiles (2016), URL above.

3 The following is informed by the old but still valuable Suzanne Keller, *The Urban Neighborhood: A Sociological Perspective*, Studies in Sociology (New York: Random House, 1968), especially chapter 2, "The Urban Neighbourhood," 77–123; Emily Talen, *Neighbourhood* (New York: Oxford University Press, 2019); and Richard Harris, *The Emergence of Neighbourhoods in Canadian Cities*, unpublished draft manuscript (the author is grateful to Professor Harris for sharing this valuable in-progress work).

4 *Merriam-Webster Unabridged Dictionary*, online edition, at https://unabridged.merriam-webster.com/

5 Lewis Mumford, "The Neighbourhood and the Neighbourhood Unit," *Town Planning Review* 24, no. 4 (January 1954): 256–70; Christopher Silver, "Neighbourhood Planning in Historical Perspective," *American Planning Association Journal* 51, no. 2 (Spring 1985): 160–74; Talen, *Neighbourhood*, 36–59.
6 Keller, *The Urban Neighbourhood*, 103, 106, 119.
7 Keller, *The Urban Neighbourhood*, 88–90.
8 Robert F. Harney, ed., *Gathering Place: People and Neighbourhoods of Toronto, 1834–1945* (Toronto: Multicultural History Society of Ontario, 1985); Annabelle Slaight, ed., *Exploring Toronto* (Toronto: Toronto Chapter of Architects, 1972); and Marjorie Harris, *Toronto: The City of Neighbourhoods* (Toronto: McClelland and Stewart, 1984), notably the short introduction by artist Harold Town.
9 Spiro Kostof, *The City Shaped: Urban Patterns and Meanings through History* (London: Thames and Hudson, 1991), 16.
10 Carolyn Whitzman, *Suburb, Slum, Urban Village: Transformations in Toronto's Parkdale Neighbourhood, 1875–2002* (Vancouver: UBC Press, 2009); Joanne Doucette, *Leslieville: Pigs, Flowers and Bricks* (self-published, 2016).
11 "Cultural Landscapes," https://whc.unesco.org/en/culturallandscape/
12 www.tclf.org/. It is also at the heart of Ann Durkin Keating, *Chicagoland: City and Suburbs in the Railroad Age* (Chicago: University of Chicago Press, 2005), which covers ground similar to that covered by this book.

1. Claiming and Founding

1 The following draws from Conrad E. Heidenreich and Robert W.C. Burgar, "Native Settlement to 1847," in *Special Places: The Changing Ecosystems of the Toronto Region*, ed. Betty I. Roots et al. (Vancouver: UBC Press, 1999), 63–75; Ronald F. Williamson, "Before the Visitors," in *Toronto: An Illustrated History of Its First 12,000 Years*, ed. Ronald F. Williamson, 25–52 (Toronto: Lorimer, 2008); Bruce G. Trigger, "The Original Iroquois: Huron, Petun, and Neutral," in *Aboriginal Ontario: Historical Perspectives on the First Nations*, ed. Edward S. Rogers and Donald B. Smith, 41–63 (Toronto: Dundurn, 1994); and Derek Hayes, *Historical Atlas of Toronto* (Vancouver: Douglas & McIntyre, 2008), 8–9.
2 Trigger, "The Original Iroquois," 41.
3 Joanne Doucette, *Leslieville: Pigs, Flowers and Bricks* (self-published, 2016), presents good examples of this, drawing mostly from old sources, in her chapter "First Nations over the Don," 3–12.
4 Jordan Stanger-Ross, "Municipal Colonialism in Vancouver: City Planning and the Conflict over Indian Reserves, 1928–1950s," *Canadian Historical Review* 89, no. 4 (2008): 541–80.
5 Heidenreich and Burgar, "Native Settlement to 1847," 74; Jon Johnson, "The Indigenous Environmental History of Toronto, 'The Meeting Place'," in *Urban Explorations: Environmental Histories of the Toronto Region*, ed. L. Anders Sandberg, 59–71 (Hamilton, ON: Wilson Institute for Canadian History, 2013).
6 Victoria Freeman, "Toronto Has No History: Indigeneity, Settler Colonialism and Historical Memory in Canada's Largest City" (PhD diss., UT, 2010).

Freeman, among others, asserts that Indigenous presence has been, and is still being, "written out" of Toronto's history.

7 A. Rodney Bobiwash, "The History of Native People in the Toronto Area," in *The Meeting Place: Aboriginal Life in Toronto*, ed. Frances Sanderson and Heather Howard-Bobiwash, 19–22 (Toronto: Native Canadian Centre of Toronto, 1997), portrays this somewhat differently. In 1881 Toronto's population officially included 6 "Indians" (none resided in St Lawrence Ward, which included the Beaches), 18 in 1901, and 48 in 1911, though many Indigenous in the city likely were not counted – Census of Canada, 1881 (table 3), 1901 (table 11), and 1911 (table 7) accessed through the UT Map and Data Library website, https://mdl.library.utoronto.ca/collections/numeric-data/census-canada/historical.

8 Robert J. Surtees, "Land Cessions, 1763–1830," in Rogers and Smith, *Aboriginal Ontario*, 101–7. The legitimacy of these treaties has long been questioned, and in recent years they have been subject to renegotiation.

9 Hayes, *Historical Atlas*, 16–27.

10 "City of Toronto and Its Liberties," by J.G. Chewett, 1834, accessed through TPL Digital Archive.

11 Among the grantees and early landowners encountered are David Ramsay, Darcy Boulton and his family, John Henry Dunn and his family, William Cayley, John Hillyard Cameron, Jean B. Bouchette, Joseph Forsyth, John Baskerville Glegg, and William Cooper, most of whom were prominent enough to be the subject of a brief, at least semi-published, biography. The most valuable source of early land ownership is the Historical Books in the Ontario Land Registry Office website, accessible at www.onland.ca/ui/.

12 From the Executive Council's order of 9 April 1799, cited by Robert R. Bonis, ed., *A History of Scarborough* (Scarborough, ON: Scarborough Public Library, 1968), 260; Bonis's recounting of the road's creation in "Old Scarborough Roads," 255–77, is definitive, explaining clearly how Danforth's Road differs from the Kingston Road; see also "Danforth, Asa," *DCB*, vol. 6.

13 G.P. de T. Glazebrook, *The Story of Toronto* (Toronto: UT Press, 1971), 114–16. "Liberties" is an ancient British term referring to land outside a city proper but still partially under the city's jurisdiction; Toronto's liberties would be fully incorporated into the city later in the century.

14 Marjorie Howard, "The History of the Beaches District," n.d. (c. 1938), handwritten essay, TPL, Beaches Branch, Scrapbook, Local History Collection.

15 *Tremaine's Map of the County of York Canada West* (Toronto: Geo. C. Tremaine, 1860), plate 11, accessed through UT Library website.

16 Mary Campbell and Barbara Myrvold, *The Beach in Pictures, 1793–1932* (Toronto: TPL Board, 1988), 34; Southeast York Township, from *Illustrated Historical Atlas of the County of York* (1878).

17 Howard, "The History of the Beaches District."

18 "Sketch Sheets of a Winter Reconnaissance of the Country East of Toronto …," 17 April 1868, accessed at http://oldtorontomaps.blogspot.com.

2. Leisure and Pleasure

1 Mary Campbell and Barbara Myrvold, *The Beach in Pictures, 1793–1932* (Toronto: TPL Board, 1988), 36–8; they draw from contemporary local newspapers.
2 *Tremaine's Map of the County of York Canada West* (Toronto: Geo. C. Tremaine, 1860); "Paterson, Peter," *DCB*, vol. 11; "Dr. Orlando Salathiel Winstanley," in William Caniff, *The Medical Profession in Upper Canada, 1783–1850* (Toronto: William Briggs, 1894).
3 C. Pelham Mulvany, *Toronto: Past and Present* (Toronto: W.E. Caiger, 1884), 102.
4 "East Toronto Notes," *Toronto World*, 27 May 1895.
5 Drawing from Campbell and Myrvold, *The Beach in Pictures*, 26, which looks to be the most reliable account of Williams and Kew Gardens.
6 OLRO, Historical Books, Book 557, p. 37, for initial purchase, and Book 255, pp. 248 and 278, for the second purchase (Blocks "T" and "U" in RP #90, for each of which Williams paid £500); accessed at www.onland.ca /ui/, folios 1 and 3.
7 John Hannigan, *Fantasy City: Pleasure and Profit in the Postmodern Metropolis* (London and New York: Routledge, 1998), 17–25.
8 *Toronto World*, 22 July 1891.
9 *The Globe*, 12 May 1880, Classified Ads, p. 1.
10 Ted Reeve, "More Beach Reminiscences," in TPL, Beaches Branch, Local History Scrapbooks.
11 Various newspaper social columns; Campbell and Myrvold, *The Beach in Pictures*, 26.
12 Campbell and Myrvold, *The Beach in Pictures*, 34–5; "Monro, George," *DCB*, vol. 10.
13 Louis H. Pursley, *Street Railways of Toronto, 1861–1921* (Los Angeles: Electric Railway Publications, 1958), 11, 16, 18; David E. Nye, "Crosstown Transfer," chapter 3 in *Electrifying America: Social Meanings of a New Technology, 1880–1940* (Cambridge, MA: MIT Press, 1990), 85–137.
14 "Hopeful for Munro Park," *Toronto World*, 22 May 1896.
15 Robert M. Stamp, *Bright Lights Big City: The History of Electricity in Toronto* (Toronto: City of Toronto, 1991), 18.
16 "East Toronto Notes," *Toronto World*, 27 May 1895.
17 "Victoria and Munro Parks," *Toronto World*, 23 May 1900.
18 "Toronto, A Summer Resort," *Toronto World*, 14 July 1900; for the phenomenon of the Ontario cottage more generally, see Julia Harrison, "An Introduction to the Cottage," *A Timeless Place: The Ontario Cottage* (Vancouver: UBC Press, 2013), 1–39.
19 "Wilson, Sir Adam," *DCB*, vol. 12 – this entry makes no mention of his Balmy Beach endeavour; see also "Sir Adam Wilson Dead," *The Globe*, 30 Dec. 1891, p. 8; "Hon. Sir Adam Wilson," *Commemorative Biographical Record of the County of York*, 277–8 (Toronto: J.H. Beers and Company, 1907), 140–2; and "Sir Adam Wilson, Knt.," *Canada Law Journal*, 23, no. 21 (1 Dec. 1887): 401–3, with details about his legal career.

20 OLRO, Historical Books, Book 557, accessed at www.onland.ca/ui /, Folios 1 and 7.

21 "Beaches Become a Populous Suburb," *Toronto Daily Star*, 21 April 1906, p. 12; OLRO, Book 557, transactions relating to Lots 1 and 2, Concessions 1 and Broken Front; "Dunn, John Henry," *DCB*, vol. 8.

22 It is shown in the *Illustrated Historical Atlas of the County of York* (Toronto: Miles & Co., 1878).

23 Its location is precisely drawn on RP #1047 (18 June 1890); Goad's Fire Insurance Plan for 1913, sheet 914, accessed through UT Map Library, and Atlas for 1924; "Conditions and Soundings – Woodbine Avenue East to City Limits," 17 July 1929, CTA, Series 724, Item 205.

24 *The Globe*, 29 April 1880, Classified, p. 1.

25 RP #406 (17 Jan. 1876); "Sale of Park Lots at Balmy Beach," *The Globe*, 7 Sept. 1878, p. 6.

26 Spiro Kostof, *The City Assembled: The Elements of Urban Form through History* (London: Thames and Hudson, 1992), 65; Anthony Sutcliffe, *Towards the Planned City: Germany, Great Britain, United States and France, 1780–1914* (New York: St. Martin's Press, 1981), 32.

27 Jon Peterson, *The Birth of City Planning in the United States, 1840–1917* (Baltimore: Johns Hopkins University Press, 2003), 47–50.

28 "The Beaches Become a Populous Suburb"; *Illustrated Historical Atlas of the County of York*, southeast portion.

29 Winstanley had possession of Lots 52 to 78: OLRO, Historical Books, Book 557, Folios 133–59, accessed at www.onland.ca/ui/

30 Biographies: "Dr. Orlando Salathiel Winstanley," in Caniff, *The Medical Profession in Upper Canada;* "Robert Beaty" and "James Beaty," *The Canadian Biographical Dictionary and Portrait Gallery of Eminent and Self-Made Men*, Ontario Volume (Toronto, Chicago, and New York: American Biographical Publishing Company, 1880), 34–41 and 424–30; "Allan MacLean Howard," *Commemorative Biographical Record of the County of York*, 277–8 (Toronto: J.H. Beers and Company, 1907). The original fourth partner was Benjamin Morton, a major developer north of Kingston Road, but he promptly sold his portion to Howard.

31 Kevin McConnell, *The History of the Balmy Beach Club* (privately published, n.d.), 18, states Winstanley's cottage was built in 1884, but does not indicate the source of this detail.

32 Marjorie Howard, "The History of the Beaches District," n.d. (c. 1938), handwritten essay, TPL, Beaches Branch, Scrapbook, Local History Collection. This now-valuable piece of ephemera includes the sketch map, based on the recollections of "Captain Jack Williams and Mr. Kew Williams," two of Joseph Williams's sons. For sandy track, see photograph, "Beech Avenue," 1885, TPL Digital Archive, PICTURES-R-5456.

33 "The Beaches Become a Populous Suburb"; Goad's Fire Insurance Plan of 1913, Sheet 914, accessed through UT Map Library; Goad's Atlas, 1924; OLRO, Book 505, Plan 406, Lots 1–52, accessed at www.onland

.ca/ui/; McConnell, *The History of the Balmy Beach Club*, 19, and other photographs in the possession of the Balmy Beach Club.

34 CTA, Series 749, ET ARs, 1889–93.

35 OLRO, Historical Books, Book 557, Folios 160 and 185–6, accessed at www.onland.ca/ui/ – four separate purchases.

36 OLRO, Historical Books, Book 675A, Sheet 5, accessed at www.onland .ca/ui/. Trout and James Beaty were business associates.

37 Auction advertisement, "John Leys Estate," *The Globe*, 7 May 1892, p. 6. A wealthy Toronto businessman by this name died in January 1892: "General News of the City," *The Globe*, 30 Jan. (p. 20) and 4 Feb. (p. 8).

38 "Balmy Beach Registered Plan 1183," *Toronto World*; CTA, Series 749, ET ARs, 1893.

39 "Personal," *The Globe*, 20 Aug. 1896, p. 12.

40 CTA, Series 749, ET AR, 1895 and 1900; RP #1178 (12 June 1895); classified advertisement, "Balmy Beach Lots for Sale Cheap," *The Globe*, 28 May 1895, p. 2.

41 Dimensions inferred from scale drawings, "Conditions and Soundings – Woodbine Avenue to East City Limits," 17 July 1929, CTA, Series 724, Item 205; "Balmy Beach Registered Plan 1183," *Toronto World*, 2 June 1900, p. 9. This advertisement includes a conceptual map showing lakefront cottages.

42 CTA, Series 749, ET ARs, 1902; RP #1236 (20 May 1902). Coatsworth's transactions are especially hard to track.

43 "The Beaches Become a Populous Suburb" states Fernwood Park belonged to Charles R. Acres in 1906. It is still labelled "Fernwood" in the 1913 Goad's Fire Insurance Plan, Sheet 913 (accessed through UT Map Library).

44 RP #1241 (24 Oct.1902); TCDs for Balsam Avenue, 1900 and 1902; CTA, Series 749, ET AR, 1902, assessed it at $1,400 but it may not have been fully built; "Conditions and Soundings – Woodbine Avenue to East City Limits," 17 July 1929, CTA, Series 724, Item 205.

45 OLRO, Historical Book 557, Plan 406, Lots 52–78.

46 RP #1047 (18 June 1890); CTA, Series 749, ET ARs, 1891.

47 CTA, Series 749, ET ARs, 1891–7; Photograph, 372 Lake Front, CTA, Series 372, Sub-series 3, Item 1181; for Ada (Winstanley) McMichael, see www .wikitree.com/wiki/McMichael-277.

48 OLRO, Book 505, Plan 406, Lots 1–52.

49 Evident in assessment photographs from 1930 to 1931 in CTA, Series 372, Sub-series 3, eg. Items 994 and 1180, as well as Item 1184, reproduced here as figure 8.

50 "Munro Park, Balmy Beach," *Toronto World*, 26 April 1899.

51 CTA, Series 749, ET ARs, 1889 and following years; in 1893 Whatmough's property (then owned by his widow) was assessed (house and land) at $2,400; both men had Toronto residences through the 1890s; Snider, whose office was downtown on King Street, is not listed as a resident of Balmy Beach until 1904 (TCDs); photograph of his house in 1972, prior to its demolition, "House, Beech Avenue, nos. 217–219 …," TPL, LOCHIST-BE-005.

52 CTA, Series 749, ET ARs, various years. Gardiner's cottage, built about 1900, is on the rough map in "Balmy Beach Registered Plan 1183"; both men are listed with Balsam Avenue as their residence in T and ET directories.
53 This draws mostly from two memoirs: Cathy Commins, "A History of Balmy Beach," *Ward 9 News*, April 1980 [and subsequent two issues], a schoolgirl's interview of her grandmother; and Mrs. Norman A. Keys, "Balmy Beach [reminiscences]," 2004 (photocopy of 1967 typescript), both held in TPL, Beaches Branch, Local History Collection.
54 "Balmy Beach Registered Plan 1183" shows location of church; John Ross Robertson, *Landmarks of Toronto* (Toronto: J. Ross Robertson, 1894), 118–19, describes but does not depict it.
55 Campbell and Myrvold, *The Beach in Pictures*, 30.
56 CTA, CT ARs, 1896, shows eleven houses in front of Kew Gardens, four owned by members of the Williams family; for leased properties, the name is sometimes the lessee, not the owner, so the Williams family might have owned more properties.
57 RPs #492 (June 1885) and #560 (April 1886); TCD, 1892 identifies Dunn as a market gardener.
58 RP #M37 (22 Dec. 1887).
59 RP# 496 (12 June 1885); a marsh line is drawn on the registered plan.
60 RP #198E (12 March 1901); the Scottish Ontario and Manitoba Land Company was the mortgagee.
61 CTA, CT ARs, and TCDs, various years.
62 Goad's Atlas, 1913; CTA, Series 372, Sub-series 3 (Assessment Photos) and 1 (Architect's Photos); "Conditions and Soundings – Woodbine Avenue to East City Limits," 17 July 1929, CTA, Series 724, Item 205.
63 CTA, CT ARs, various years.
64 Campbell and Myrvold, *The Beach in Pictures*, 10.
65 Coatsworth, a future mayor, did create a small Kew Beach subdivision just back from the lake (see ahead).
66 *Kew Beach United Church, Toronto, 1882–1942: The Story of Our Church* (privately published, n.d., 1943?), TPL, Beaches Branch, Local History Collection; Gunn's cottage is visible in the photograph, CTA, Series 372, Sub-series 7, Item 59; generally: assessment photographs of houses prior to 1930 expropriation – CTA, Series 372, Sub-series 3, Item 804 and many others.
67 *Toronto World*, 4 July 1898.
68 "Fresh Air Fund," *The Globe*, 29 Aug. 1898, p. 7. Philip G. Mackintosh and Richard Anderson, "The Toronto Star Fresh Air Fund: Transcendental Rescue in a Modern City, 1900–1915," *Geographical Review* 99 (4): 539–62, date the creation of the FAF as summer 1901 (p. 544), so this would have been a preliminary, informal fundraiser.
69 "Dumped in the Ditch," *The Evening Star*, 21 July 1897, p. 1; "The Beaches Become a Populous Suburb" notes persistent disdain for Munro Park among Balmy Beachers.

70 Photographs of original clubhouses are "Beaches Park ...;" 1916, TPL, PICTURES-R-3561 (for Kew) and "Balmy Beach Club ...," 1900 [incorrect date], TPL, PICTURES-R-5449 (for Balmy).
71 "At The Beaches," *Toronto Daily Star*, 15 Aug. 1903, p. 15.
72 Commins, "A History of Balmy Beach" (second instalment), describes The Pines and an ancillary building of two-storey family rental units called Pine Terrace on Beech Avenue north of Queen Street; a large building erected on that site in 1900 had a commercial as well as a residential assessment applied starting 1905 – CTA, Series 749, ET ARs, 1902 and 1905.
73 TCDs, Fisherman's Island and Woodbine Beach, various years; CTA, Series 769, Files 28–32 contain hundreds of letters to and from residents; CTCMs, 1902, R29 of Property Cttee gives background.
74 The City accepted tenders for improving the street in 1888 (R15 [24 July 1888] and R20 [2 Oct. 1888] of Cttee of Works, CTCMs, 1888), but neither the TSR nor the TRC found the work, if it was done, satisfactory for they did not extend service; the TRC later laid temporary track, and provided service off and on, but not until 1893, when the City laid "permanent pavement," did it commence full service to the city limit – R37 of Cttee of Works, CTCMs, 1893, 630, and earlier reports; the official date for the extension is 1893 – Pursley, *Street Railways of Toronto*, 18, 42, 44.
75 TPL, Beaches Branch, Local History Scrapbooks: Churches.
76 "Munro Park, Balmy Beach," *Toronto World*, 26 Apr. 1899; "Down at the Beaches," *The Evening Star*, 4 May 1899.
77 "Toronto: A Summer Resort," *Toronto World*, 14 July 1900.

3. Suburb Building

1 For a concise overview of this, internationally, see Spiro Kostof, *The City Assembled: The Elements of Urban Form through History* (London: Thames and Hudson, 1992), 62–5.
2 Noted in Kenneth T. Jackson, *Crabgrass Frontier: The Suburbanization of the United States* (New York: Oxford University Press, 1985), 74.
3 Provincial surveyors realigned the original Queen Street when they rebuilt it in 1887, but still gave no consideration to the street's future function – RP #620 (12 June 1885).
4 This was said in 1912 about the Montreal suburb of Mount Royal; cited in Larry McCann, "Planning and Building the Corporate Suburb of Mount Royal, 1910–1925," *Planning Perspectives* 11 (1996): 269.
5 "An Act Respecting Registrars, etc.," *Statutes of Ontario*, 29 Victoria (1867), Chapter 20, Section 75.
6 CT Bylaw #6907 (23 Feb. 1914), CTCMs, 1914, 68, sets a building line for Lee Avenue, minimum 16 feet from the street on the east side and 10 feet on the west; the City was acting under the provincial Municipal Act of 1913, which gave cities the authority to set minimum (not specific) setbacks on streets; in fact, "The Municipal Amendment Act," *Statutes of*

Ontario, 4 Edward VII (1904), Chapter 22, Section 19 already empowered it to do this, but the City did not until after the passage of the 1913 Act.

7 "An Act Respecting Municipal Institutions," *Revised Statutes of Ontario*, 1887, Chapter 184, Section 545.

8 Anthony Sutcliffe, *Towards the Planned City: Germany, Great Britain, United States and France, 1780–1914* (New York: St. Martin's Press, 1981), 19–35; Brian Ladd, "City Extension Planning," Chapter 3 in *Urban Planning and Civic Order in Germany, 1860–1914* (Cambridge: Harvard University Press, 1990).

9 Isobel K. Ganton, "Land Subdivision in Toronto, 1851–1883," in *Shaping the Urban Landscape: Aspects of the Canadian City-Building Process*, ed. Gilbert A. Stelter and Alan F.J. Artibise (Ottawa: Carleton University Press, 1982), 200–31.

10 For the Beaty brothers, RP #1183 (18 Feb. 1895), and advertisement, "Balmy Beach Registered Plan 1183," *Toronto World*, 2 June 1900, p. 9. Their partner was John Latimer Kerr (1854–1929); James Beaty's interest was in the hands of his wife Fanny; for Howard, RP #1216 (surveyed 1897, registered 1900).

11 Ontario Land Records Office, Historical Books, accessed at www.onland.ca/ui/ (hereafter OLRO), Book 557, Plan 406, Lots 63–72; "Fleming, Robert John," *DCB*, vol. 15; RP #733 (25 April 1887).

12 OLRO, Book 505, Plan 406, Lots 20–5; RP #732 (4 May 1887).

13 OLRO, Book 505, Plan 406, Lots 27–33; RP #1038 (6 June 1890). After fifteen years RP#1038 was revised by Wilson's nieces and nephews – he had no children – with no mention of his wife, who was still alive (d. 1906), or Mrs. Barnett – RP #1286 (4 Feb. 1905); his cottage stood, untended and usually vacant, until demolished in 1931.

14 For $42,400 – OLRO, Book 505, Plan 406, passim; RP #1064 (26 Sept. 1890).

15 "Beaches Become a Populous Suburb," *Toronto Daily Star*, 21 April 1906, p. 12, states that Balmy Beach lots had to have a frontage of at least 50 feet and its houses a value of at least a $2,000; who or what required this is left unsaid, but this requirement, if it existed, was clearly not being enforced – a run of good-sized semi-detached houses on the east side of Willow Avenue, built by a reputable builder about 1908 on 20-foot lots, were assessed at $1,200, and an adjacent detached house, on a 50-foot lot, at $1600 – CT ARs, 1910.

16 Goad's Atlas, 1913.

17 RP #1216 (surveyed 1897, registered 1900); CTA, ARs for Balsam Avenue in the 1890s; Goad's Atlas, 1913.

18 Goad's Atlas, 1913 and 1924.

19 Raphaël Fischler, "Development Controls in Toronto in the Nineteenth Century," *Urban History Review* 36, no. 1 (Fall 2007): 16–31; "An Act Respecting Municipal Institutions," *Revised Statutes of Ontario*, 1887, Chapter 184, Section 545. It remained essentially unchanged a decade later, *RSO*, 1897, Chapter 223, Section 630 (2).

20 Russell Snow was councillor – CTA, Fonds 204, Series 1000. These eccentricities seem to underlie a request for making the area a

historical conservation district: ERA Architects, "Balmy Beach Heritage Conservation District, Glenfern Area (DRAFT)," 6 June 2006.

21 RP #1183 (18 Feb. 1895).

22 CTD for 1900 shows 513 residents of East Toronto, of which 234 were GTR employees; only eight residents of Balmy Beach were recorded in the directory, and none of them worked for the GTR.

23 "Beaches Become a Populous Suburb," *Toronto Daily Star*, 21 April 1906, p. 12.

24 The annexation was reviewed and approved by the Ontario Railway and Municipal Board on 29 Sept. 1908, effective 15 Dec. 1908; Toronto listed the terms in Minute 441, 14 July 1908, CTCMs, 1908, 219.

25 Mary Campbell and Barbara Myrvold, *The Beach in Pictures*, 1793–1932 (Toronto: TPL Board, 1988), 12, drawing from *Toronto World*.

26 "An Act Respecting the Town of East Toronto and Balmy Beach Park," *Statutes of Ontario*, 3 Edward VII (1903), Chapter 50. The statute's preamble recounts the history.

27 The City of Toronto questioned this but let it stand. Typescript, "History of Balmy Beach Park" (dated "193?"), CTA, Series 487, File 495; R1 of Cttee on Legislation and Reception, CTCMs, 1910, 103.

28 Goad's Atlas, 1884; Director's Report, 1886, with a list of shareholders, on Internet Archive: https://openlibrary.org/authors/OL7193343A/Scottish_Ontario_and_Manitoba_Land_Company_(Ltd.).

29 RP #496 (12 June 1885).

30 "Ewart (Euart), John," *DCB*, vol. 8; Tremaine Map (1860) has Ewart as owner; *Illustrated Historical Atlas of the County of York* (Toronto: Miles & Co., 1878), southeast portion, shows James McClennan, QC (soon to be a Chief Justice) as owner; Goad's Atlas 1884 shows Ewart *estate* as owner.

31 RP #M37 (22 Dec. 1887); RP #M28 (13 Sept. 1887).

32 RP #90 (1854), with park lots ranging from five to fifteen acres; "A Plan of Lot No. 4 … to be sold by auction … 30th June 1853," CTA, Fonds 79, Series 346, File 62.

33 "Lee, Walter Sutherland," *DCB*, vol. 13; Lee is owner in Goad's Atlas 1890 but not 1884.

34 RP #898 (25 Apr. 1889) and RP #984 (28 Oct. 1889).

35 *Illustrated Historical Atlas of the County of York*; family history from www.wikitree.com/wiki/Howard-15052; Howard's first transactions are Feb. 1876 – OLRO, Book 557, Concession 1, Lot 3, Folio 28.

36 AMH Sr. is on record selling a large, unspecified, block of land south of Queen Street to AMH Jr. for $10,000 in 1888 – OLRO, Book 675A, Sheet 7.

37 CTA, ARs, 1890s.

38 "The Beaches Become a Populous Suburb," *Toronto Daily Star*, 21 April 1906, p. 12. The House was designed by Toronto architect C.F. Wagner.

39 RP #254E (14 Sept. 1904).

40 OLRO, Book 557, Concession 1, Lot 3, Folio 21.

41 Hambly, RP #M238 (14 Dec. 1905); Islesworth and Hammersmith appear on, but are not part of, RP #315 (2 March 1910) – Williams seems not to have registered his subdivisions; Kenilworth, RP #M218 (28 July 1903).

42 RPs #1408 (7 April 1908) and #389E (28 Jan. 1910) created 50-foot lots on both streets south of Queen; RP #502E (3 Sept.1913) created 30-foot lots on Neville Park north of Queen.
43 Goad's Atlas, 1913; Nik Luka, "From Summer Cottage Colony to Metropolitan Suburb: Toronto's Beach District, 1889–1929," *Urban History Review* 35, no. 1 (Fall 2006): 23–4.
44 Rough visual count of the Goad's Atlas, 1913, but individual dwellings are sometimes hard to discern.
45 Household size: "The Shift to Smaller Households over the Last Century," Chart 1, on Statistics Canada website: https://www150.statcan.gc.ca/n1/pub/11-630-x/11-630-x2015008-eng.htm.
46 Consistent with Luka, "From Summer Cottage Colony to Metropolitan Suburb."
47 Richard Harris, "The Making of American Suburbs, 1900–1950: A Reconstruction," in *Changing Suburbs: Foundation, Form and Function*, ed. Richard Harris and Peter Larkham (London: E & FN Spon, 1999), 91–110. Harris observes this occurring outside incorporated areas, but this was within Toronto's boundaries; Sam Bass Warner, *Streetcar Suburbs: The Process of Growth in Boston (1870–1900)* (Cambridge, MA: Harvard University Press, 1962), 52–64.
48 Warner, *Streetcar Suburbs*, 49–52; Louis H. Pursley, *Street Railways of Toronto, 1861–1921* (Los Angeles: Electric Railway Publications, 1958), 42 notes increasing service 1898–1908.
49 Appendix, table 3. A few worked in other locations served by the streetcar.
50 Warner, *Streetcar Suburbs*, 117–19.
51 Warner, *Streetcar Suburbs*, 75.
52 Warner, *Streetcar Suburbs*, 125–36, quotation 129.
53 Derek Hayes, *Historical Atlas of Toronto* (Vancouver: Douglas & McIntyre, 2008), 114–17; Ron Fischer, "The Development of the Garden Suburb in Toronto," *Journal of Garden History* 3, no. 3 (1983): 193–207.
54 Toronto overall did have a significant minority of Roman Catholics (15%) in 1911, but few settled in the Beaches – see table 7 in J.M.S. Careless, *Toronto to 1918: An Illustrated History* (Toronto: Lorimer, 1984), 201; the Beaty and Snow families, among the founders of Balmy Beach, were adherents of the dissenting Disciples of Christ sect, James and Robert having been brought into it by their strong-willed uncle James Beaty – "Beaty, James," *DCB*, vol. 12.
55 "The Municipal Amendment Act 1904," *Statutes of Ontario*, 4 Edward VII (1904), Chapter 22, Section 19; CT Bylaw #6061 (13 May 1912); see chapter 4.
56 Appendix, table 1.
57 This interpretation is often attributed to Warner's *Streetcar Suburbs*, although Warner (chapter 5, "The Weave Small Patterns," 67–116) observed lower-middle-class residents in his study area; discussed in Richard Harris, *Creeping Conformity: How Canada Became Suburban, 1900–1950* (Toronto: University of Toronto Press, 2004), 18–22; and Emily Talen, *Neighbourhood* (New York: Oxford University Press, 2019), 32–3.

58 Appendix, table 1.
59 Kenneth Norrie and Douglas Owram, *A History of the Canadian Economy*, 2nd ed. (Toronto: Harcourt Brace Canada, 1996), 268–73; Ian M. Drummond, "The Development of Industrial Cities," chapter 10 in *Progress without Planning: The Economic History of Ontario from Confederation to the Second World War* (Toronto: UT Press, 1987).

4. The Suburb and the City

1 Appendix of Statistical Tables in J.M.S. Careless, *Toronto to 1918: An Illustrated History* (Toronto: Lorimer, 1984), 200–3; 1914 population is from TCD, 1915.
2 Calculated from Careless, *Toronto to 1918*, table 6, 203.
3 Although still covered in most history textbooks, this movement has not been subject to much new analytical research in English Canada for many years; articles assembled by Stelter and Artibise in the 1970s remain foundational: *The Canadian City: Essays in Urban History*, ed. Gilbert A. Stelter and Alan F.J. Artibise (Toronto: McClelland & Stewart, 1977), and *The Usable Urban Past: Planning and Politics in the Modern Canadian City*, ed. Gilbert A. Stelter and Alan F.J. Artibise (Toronto: McClelland & Stewart, 1979).
4 CTA, Series 1282, City Engineer's Reports, 1897 and 1911.
5 "Annexation Map," CTA, Series 727, Item 122 (accessible on CTA website).
6 Appendix, table 3.
7 Numbers in this paragraph were calculated by author from Census of Canada, 1911, vol. 1, table 9, and vol. 2, tables 4, 7, 15, and 16; the census identifies Canadian-born but counts them as British-born, and identifies British Isles–born but does not count them as foreign-born; as such, the census data was recalculated for the point explored here.
8 Census of Canada, 1901, vol. 1, table 11 (Toronto East, Ward 1). This is consistent with Lillian Petroff, "Sojourner and Settler: The Macedonian Presence in the City, 1903–1940," in *Gathering Place: Peoples and Neighbourhoods of Toronto, 1834–1945*, ed. Robert F. Harney, 177–203 (Toronto: Multicultural History Society of Ontario, 1985).
9 R1 of the Cttee of Parks and Exhibitions, CTCMs, 1906, 74; and "Bylaw to Expropriate Lands on Leuty Avenue for Park Purposes," rejected 22 Oct. 1906, CTCMs, 1906, 1384.
10 CT Bylaw #4896, 25 March 1907, CTCMs, 1907, 292–3.
11 R5 of the Cttee of Parks and Exhibitions in R9 of the BC, 25 March 1907, CTCMs, 1907, 365–7; also; R10 of the BC, CTCMs, 1907, 369–71.
12 Goad's Atlas; 1913 shows the new residential streets but no subdivision plan numbers.
13 Assessment Commissioner's report in R9 of the BC, 25 March 1907, CTCMs, 1907, 365–7.
14 Letter, 4 April 1907, Assessment Commissioner to Mayor and Council, in R10 of the BC, CTCMs, 1907, 370; Williams's residence at 40 Lee Avenue is listed in the 1909 TCD but not the 1910 TCD.

15 CTCMs, 1908, numerous references to buying out lots and leases, and CTCMs, 1909, for selling cottages intact; documents about removing and demolishing the cottages are in CTA, Fonds 200, Series 483, File 37.
16 R3 of the BC adopted 24 Feb. 1908; offprints of this and several other relevant pages from the minutes are in CTA, Fonds 200, Series 483, File 38.
17 R11 of Cttee on Parks and Exhibitions, CTCMs, 1908, 860–1 for name of park and initial budget for improvements (later increased by $1,200).
18 CTA, various photographs in Fonds 200, Series 372, Subseries 52, especially Item 367.
19 CTA, Series 1282, City Engineer's Reports, various years.
20 "Turning on Toronto: A History of Toronto Hydro," online web exhibit, CTA website. Creation of the municipal system is recounted in the "Explanatory Memorandum" at the front of the Toronto Hydro-Electric System Annual Report, 1911–12 (CTA).
21 CTA, Series 1282, City Engineer's Reports, various years; the definitive history of the early waterworks, with full engineering details, is City of Toronto, Board of Commissioners, "Report upon the Existing Water Works System," 1912 (CTA); Elwood Jones and Douglas McCalla, "Toronto Waterworks, 1840–77: Continuity and Change in Nineteenth-Century Toronto Politics," *Canadian Historical Review* 60, no. 3 (1979): 300–23.
22 CTA, Series 1282, City Engineer's Report, 1900, 71.
23 "An Act Respecting the Town of East Toronto," *Statutes of Ontario*, 8 Edward VII (1908), Chapter 79, Schedule A; "The Beaches Become a Populous Suburb," *Toronto Daily Star*, 21 April 1906, p. 12; Goad's Fire Insurance Plan for 1913, sheet 906, accessed through UT Map Library.
24 CTCMs, 1908, Minute 441, 14 July 1908; CTA, Series 1282, City Engineer's Report, 1909.
25 Mrs. Norman A. Keys, "Balmy Beach [reminiscences]," 2004 (photocopy of 1967 typescript), TPL, Beaches Branch, Local History Collection, 1; Glen Cochrane and Jean Cochrane, *The Beach: An Illustrated History from the Lake to Kingston Road* (Toronto: ECW Press, 2009), 6.
26 CTA, Series 1282, City Engineer's Reports, 1906, 164, and 1907, 186; photos of facility CTA, Fonds 200, Series 376, File 5, Items 51 and 74.
27 "The Beaches Become a Populous Suburb," *Toronto Daily Star*, 21 April 1906, p. 12; Mrs. Norman A. Keys, "Balmy Beach [reminiscences]," 1.
28 "East Toronto Drainage System District C," R17 of the Cttee of Works, CTCMs, 1912, 1253–4.
29 Catherine Brace, "Public Works in a Canadian City: The Provision of Sewers in Toronto, 1873–1913," *Urban History Review* 23, no. 2 (March 1995): 33–43.
30 CTA, Series 1282, City Engineer's Reports, 1906, 167–8 and 1909, 222.
31 Letter, Commissioner of Works to Mayor and Council, 18 Dec. 1912, in R34 of BC, CTCMs, 1912, 1933; photo of construction, CTA, Series 372, Subseries 59, Item 113; Goad's Atlas, 1913, shows location of lakefront sewer.
32 The legal basis for these charges, initially in the *Municipal Act*, was confirmed in the *Local Improvement Act*, 2 George V (1911), Chapter 44,

in *Revised Statutes of Ontario*, 1914, Chapter 193; the background of the principle, and its application in the United States, is explained in Stephen Diamond, "The Death and Transfiguration of Benefit Taxation Special Assessments in Nineteenth-Century America," *Journal of Legal Studies* 21, no. 2 (June 1983): 201–40; CTA, Annual Report of the City Engineer, 1908.

33 Brian Ladd, *Urban Planning and Civic Order in Germany, 1870–1914* (Cambridge: Harvard University Press, 1990), 187–95.

34 "The Municipal Amendment Act 1904," *Statutes of Ontario*, 4 Edward VII (1904), Chapter 22, Section 19; Peter W. Moore, "Zoning and Planning: The Toronto Experience, 1904–1970," in Arbitise and Stelter, *The Usable Urban Past*, 316–41.

35 "The Municipal Amendment Act 1912," *Statutes of Ontario*, 3 George V (1912), Chapter 40, Section 10.

36 CT Bylaw #6061 (13 May 1912); Richard Dennis, "Interpreting the Apartment House: Modernity and Metropolitanism in Toronto, 1900–1930," *Journal of Historical Geography* 20, no. 3 (July 1994): 305–22.

37 Raphaël Fischler, "Development Controls in Toronto in the Nineteenth Century," *Urban History Review* 36, no. 1 (Fall 2007): 16–31.

38 CT Bylaw #627 (9 April 1874); Map, "City of Toronto Compiled from Surveys Made to the Present Date, 1874," accessed at TPL Digital Archive.

39 CT Bylaws #2468 (1890), #4408 (1904), and #6401 (1913); the oft-repeated claim that Toronto introduced fire controls in response to its 1904 fire has no basis in fact; the 1904 bylaw had been under development for several years.

40 CT Bylaw #2468 (1890), Section 72.

41 CT Bylaw #4408 (1904), Section CL, 96; "roughcast" is a crude form of plastering.

42 Goad's Atlas, 1910. Such houses were always identified as "wooden-framed," a somewhat misleading label because their critical feature was exterior wood cladding, not interior wood framing; houses with brick exteriors, whether structural brick or just brick cladding, usually had interior wood framing.

43 Inglewood was designed in partnership with R.J. Edwards, photograph in *Canadian Architect and Builder*, Dec. 1901; Summer House for George A. White, Item 403, "Toronto Architectural Eighteen Club Catalogue," 1902, TPL, Baldwin Collection.

44 Eg. CTA, Series 372, Sub-series 3, Items 759 (4 Kippendavie) and 795 (22 Waverley), both of which first appear in TCDs 1905.

45 CT Bylaw #4408 (1904), Section CL, 96. The bylaw states, with a confusing double negative, that the brick requirement does not apply to buildings "not over thirty-five feet in height from the ground floor to the highest point of the roof."

46 Richard Harris, "The Impact of Building Controls on Residential Development in Toronto," *Planning Perspectives* 6 (1991): 277; "Toronto's Building Bylaws," *The Canadian Engineer*, 13 Oct.1910, 484 (cited by Harris).

47 Goad's Atlas, 1913. Newer brick-clad houses are apparent in photographs of the Kew Beach area in the 1930s, e.g., CTA, Series 372, Sub-series 3, Items 787 and 789.

48 RP #M238 (14 Dec. 1905); Goad's Atlas, 1913; rough visual count by author from Goad's Atlas.
49 TCDs show no houses on these streets in 1906, house-building underway in 1908 and 1909, and essentially complete in 1912.
50 There is a cynical aphorism in present-day planning that "development follows the pipe," not the plan.
51 CT Bylaw #2468 (1890), Section 36.
52 CT Bylaw #4408 (1904), Section 33, Items 9 and 10.
53 "Mr. Dennison is building a substantial house on a brick foundation" in "Munro Park, Balmy Beach," *Toronto World*, 26 April 1899; CTA, Series 749, ET ARs, shows substantial houses on west side of Balsam Avenue after 1900, most of which are still standing; Goad's Atlas, 1913, shows most newer housing was made of brick.
54 Jane Jacobs, *Systems of Survival: A Dialogue on the Moral Foundations of Commerce and Politics* (New York: Random House, 1992); Larry McCann, "Planning and Building the Corporate Suburb of Mount Royal, 1910–1925," *Planning Perspectives* 11 (1996): 259–301, makes a similar observation.

5. Filling the Gaps

1 The City later added planning to the responsibilities of the City Surveyor but hired no trained planners; Richard White, *Planning Toronto: The Planners, the Plans, Their Legacies, 1940–80* (Vancouver, UBC Press, 2016), 23–7.
2 Ron Williams, *Landscape Architecture in Canada* (Montreal and Kingston: McGill-Queen's University Press, 2014), part 3.
3 "City and Suburbs Plans Act," 2 George V (1912), Chapter 43, Sections 3 and 4, *Revised Statutes of Ontario*, 1914, Chapter 104.
4 "Bouchette, Jean-Baptiste," *DCB*, vol. 5; Ontario Land Registry Office, Historical Books, accessed at www.onland.ca/ui/ (hereafter OLRO), Book 557, Lot 3, Concession 1; *Tremaine's Map of the County of York Canada West* (Toronto: Geo. C. Tremaine 1860); "Boulton, D'Arcy," *DCB*, vol. 6 "Boulton, Henry John," *DCB*, vol. 9; Leith Obituary – *The Canadian Law Journal* 35, no. 8 (15 April 1899): 256.
5 Generally, Mary Campbell and Barbara Myrvold, *The Beach in Pictures, 1793–1932* (Toronto: TPL Board, 1988), 30–2.
6 As of 1853, Darling also served as assistant minister of the much more important Church of the Holy Trinity in central Toronto; the incumbent there, Henry Scadding, was ailing, and Darling handled much of the day-to-day work, but it is not clear how this affected his status within the church, or his remuneration; Scadding did not relinquish his post until 1875 – "Scadding, Henry," *DCB*, vol. 13; Joseph Williams later acquired some of the southwestern portion and Allan Maclean Howard some of the southeastern portion of the property – *Illustrated Historical Atlas of the County of York* (Toronto: Miles & Co., 1878).
7 "To Be Let, Furnished, 'Glen Stewart', Norway," classified advertisement, *The Globe*, 3 August 1881. Interested parties were to apply at the house.

8 Campbell and Myrvold, *The Beach in Pictures*, 30, suggest that Frank had designed the house. A younger son Walter (1855–1892) owned other parts of the property – CTA, Series 749, ET AR, 1890.
9 "East Toronto," *Toronto Daily Star*, 27 Apr 1901, p. 7; "Ames, Alfred Ernest," *DCB*, vol. 16; "Cox, George Albertus," *DCB*, vol. 14.
10 Campbell and Myrvold, *The Beach in Pictures*, 31.
11 "A Sensation in the Business World," *Toronto Daily Star*, 2 June 1903, p. 1; photographs of the house are *Toronto Daily Star*, 10 May 1905, p. 5, and Campbell and Myrvold, *The Beach in Pictures*, 31; thanks to Joanne Doucette for introducing me to these newspaper sources.
12 "A Sensation in the Business World," *Toronto Daily Star*, 2 June 1903, p. 1; "Ames Plan Fails, Another Offered," *Toronto Daily Star*, 11 Jan. 1904, p. 7.
13 *Toronto Daily Star*, 28 Jan. 1904, p. 7, mentions this once but reports nothing further; Scott Burk and Joanne Doucette, *Toronto's Lost Golf Courses: How the Game of Golf Shaped a City, Volume 1: 1869–1919* (Toronto: Barlow Books, 2019), 214, asserts that Ames made the offer; the offer is not mentioned in city council records.
14 CTA, CT ARs show the house owned by Ames in 1904 but by Cox in 1908; intervening years were not examined.
15 "Where Earl Grey Will Spend Race Week in Toronto," *Toronto Daily Star*, 10 May 1905, p. 5; Campbell and Myrvold, *The Beach in Pictures*, 30, say both years.
16 Ted Reeves recalled that "Ames Bush" was the local name of the property in "More Beach Reminiscences," in TPL, Beaches Branch, Local History Scrapbooks.
17 OLRO, Toronto Section S, Parcel 1 (Folios 1–4) and 2 (Folios 9–14).
18 RP #315 (2 March 1910).
19 *Toronto Daily Star* in the fall of 1912: 16 Aug. p. 9, 1 Oct. p. 7, 5 Oct. p. 9, 8 Oct. pp. 7 and 9, and 11 Oct. p. 4; withdrawal of offer BC R23, CTCMs, 1912, 1535.
20 Ownership of the land around and west of the house changed from Cox to National Trust in 1909 and from National Trust to Ames in 1911 – CTA, CT ARs, 1909–11.
21 ARs show Ames's property at 10.11 acres – CTA, CT ARs 1911–14.
22 "Senator G.A. Cox Left an Estate Totaling $870,071," *Toronto Daily Star*, 14 Feb. 1914, p. 1; "Ames, Alfred Ernest," *DCB*, vol. 16.
23 "Humber Valley Annual a 'Hummer'," *Canadian Golfer* 10, no. 8 (Dec. 1924): 622, and "Glen Stewart in Play," *Canadian Golfer* 7, no. 1 (May 1921): 52, accessed at https://canadiangolfer.golfcanada.ca/. Ames continued owning the property, and his gardeners maintained the course. Its annual fee was $15, its entrance was at Stop #6 of the Kingston Road streetcar, and in 1921 it had 250 members and a waiting list.
24 "A.E. Ames Dies Banker, Broker, and Philosopher," *Toronto Daily Star*, 21 Sept. 1934, p. 1.
25 OLRO, Toronto Section S, Parcel 365, folio 746.
26 "Cox, George Albertus," *DCB*, vol. 14.

27 "Alfred Herbert Cox," J.E. Middleton, *The Municipality of Toronto A History*, vol. 3 (Toronto and New York: Dominion Publishing, 1923), 325.
28 "Howard Burlingham Dunington-Grubb" and "Lorrie Dunington-Grubb," *Canadian Encyclopedia*; Williams, *Landscape Architecture in Canada*, 302–3; Ann Milovsoroff, "'For the Love of Gardens': A Biography of H.B. and L.A. Dunington-Grubb," *Canadian Horticultural History* 2, no. 3 (1990): 101–33. These do not mention the Stewart Manor work.
29 Blueprint, "Glen Stewart, The Provident Investment Company, Toronto," undated, CTA, Series 724, Item 11; Pleasance Crawford, "Chronology for Harries, Hall, and Cruise," 29 March 2013, accessed at www.kaufmancrawford.ca/publications/HH&K%20chronology.pdf.
30 RP #M390 (27 Oct. 1913); both Provident Investment Company and Toronto Savings and Loan Co. are named as owners; plans for other parts of RP #315 were registered later.
31 OLRO, Toronto Section S, Parcel 1, folio 15; Cox family details from *Who's Who in Canada* (F.W. Cox – vol. 6/7, 1915–16; A.H. Cox – vol. 15, 1921).
32 OLRO, Toronto Section S, Parcel 4, folios 24–5 – the agreement between the City and TS&L was 6 Oct. 1913; approval is "Acceptance of Plans," BC R23, CTCMs, 1913, 1353–4.
33 Advertisements in *Toronto Daily Star*, 22 and 29 May 1914; and on 7, 11, 14, 21, and 28 March 1924; Goad's Atlas, 1913 and 1924.
34 The covenants were registered 25 August 1915 at the request of Provident Investment Company for all lots in Plan M390, excluding ten that had already been sold – OLRO, Toronto Section S, Parcel 365, Folios 749–51. They applied only to physical features, not to any race, class, or religion.
35 *Toronto Daily Star*, 14 March 1924, p. 9.
36 Photographs of newly built houses in the newspaper advertisements show mature trees.
37 R of Cttee on Parks and Exhibitions, CTCMs, 1931, 134–5; the matter had been under discussion for two years.
38 OLRO, Book 675A, Broken Front Concession, Lot 3.
39 Details from WikiTree, which cites published sources: www.wikitree.com/wiki/Grahame-50.
40 TCDs, various years; O'Connor is listed at 197–99 King Street East as a grocer and flour merchant in 1859, as wine and liquor merchant in 1868, to which is added in 1875 "Importer of Dunville & Co.'s Old Irish Whiskey" from Belfast; CTA, CT ARs, various years.
41 Campbell and Myrvold, *The Beach in Pictures*, 9, uses this name.
42 CTA, CT AR, 1885 notes a first-class brick building, 36 x 39 feet, assessed at $4,000 (comparable to the assessed value of the large lakefront summer homes erected in Balmy Beach ten years later).
43 CTA, CT ARs, 1885 and 1887, are especially detailed; Goad's Atlas, 1884, shows buildings on the property.
44 Diane Bisson, *Compassion Builds a House: The Legacy of Caring at Providence Centre* (Toronto: Providence Centre, 2000), 45–6; also www.csj-to.ca/history.

45 OLRO, Book 675A, Broken Front Concession, Lot 3, p. 4; Bisson (above) says $150,000; the purchaser was Harry A. Dorsey, who within a few months sold it to "The Toronto Park Company Ltd.," later revealed to be owned by the Toronto Railway Company.

46 Campbell and Myrvold, *The Beach in Pictures*, 27–9; "Scarboro Beach," advertisement, *Toronto World*, 27 May 1907, lists the attractions.

47 The TRC had had insufficient electricity supply until 1907, when it procured a nearly unlimited supply of Niagara hydroelectricity, possibly influencing its decision to build the larger new amusement park – Louis H. Pursley, *Street Railways of Toronto 1861–1921* (Los Angeles: Electric Railway Publications, 1958), 22 and 26; David E. Nye, *Electrifying America: Social Meanings of a New Technology, 1880–1940* (Cambridge, MA: MIT Press, 1990), 122–32.

48 Cathy Commins, "A History of Balmy Beach," *Ward 9 News*, April 1980 (3rd instalment), and Mrs. Norman A. Keys, "Balmy Beach [reminiscences]," 2004 (photocopy of 1967 typescript), both in TPL, Beaches Branch, Local History Collection; photograph, "Canoeing, Scarboro Beach Park," CTA, Fonds 1244, Item 161.

49 "The Beaches Become a Populous Suburb," *Toronto Daily Star*, 21 April 1906, p. 12.

50 "The Toronto Railway Company in Liquidation," *Toronto Daily Star*, 10 March 1925, p. 11.

51 "Transfer Scarboro Beach," *Toronto Daily Star*, 13 Nov. 1925, p. 3; BC R, CTCMs, 1925, 920; OLRO, Book 675A, Broken Front Concession, Lot 3, p. 5.

52 RP #M490 (4 Sept. 1925); A.H. Cox and R.H. Saunders signed for Provident, the latter would be elected mayor in 1945.

53 Advertisements placed by the "Scarboro Beach Home Builders" list ten separate builders, *Toronto Daily Star*, 23 Sept. 1926, p. 33; "Homeseekers Zeal Leads to Wrecking of Amusement Park," *The Globe*, 30 April 1926, paints a vivid picture of the park's transformation.

54 Advertisements have photographs of the house types for sale, e.g., *Toronto Daily Star*, 23 Sept. 1926, p. 33, and 30 Sept. 1926, p. 20.

55 *The Globe*, 2 July 1928, pp. 10–12, is a multi-page feature on Price Brothers and this undertaking; for Harry Stevens, "Price Bros' Buyer Is Harry Stevens," p. 12; for description of rental units, "Roofed with Brantford Super-Tites," p. 10.

56 Hubbard Boulevard saw the Ramona Apartments completed 1929, and the Somersby Apartments and Hubbard Park Apartments 1930 – TCDs, 1929 and 1930, and CTA, CT ARs, various years.

57 Buildings did have to be for residential use – R20 of Cttee on Property, CTCMs, 1925, 1552.

58 CTA, Fonds 444 (papers of the Baldwin and Greene architecture firm), Series 2387, File 19, includes several buildings erected by Cox and Best.

59 CT Bylaw 6061 (13 May 1912).

60 R15 of the Cttee of Property, CTCMs, 1926, 1378.

61 CTCMs, 1920–9, index entries for "apartment houses."

62 They were the construction contractors and likely also the developers (i.e., property owners) since they applied for the bylaw exemption. They sought exemption from CT Bylaw #8092 (7 April 1919), which applied to an area not included in the earlier Bylaw #6061, cited above.
63 R5 of Cttee on Property, CTCMs, 1925, 500 (for 85 Beech); and R5 of Cttee on Property, CTCMs, 1928, 483 (for 125–27 Kenilworth).
64 This observation is based on maybe a dozen such cases in CTCMs, 1920–9.
65 R17 of the Cttee of Property, CTCMs, 1925, 1531–2; Goad's Atlas, 1924.

6. The Lost Beach

1 Ted Reeve, "More Beach Reminiscences," in TPL, Beaches Branch, Scrapbooks, Local History Collection, expresses this sentiment.
2 The Toronto Harbour Commissioners, *Toronto Waterfront Development, 1912–1920* (Toronto 1912).
3 This plan is explored in Michael Moir, "Planning for Change: Harbour Commissions, Civil Engineers, and Large-Scale Manipulation of Nature," 23–47, and in Gene Desfor, Lucian Vesalon, and Jennifer Laidley, "Establishing the Toronto Harbour Commission and Its 1912 Waterfront Development Plan," 47–74, in *Reshaping Toronto's Waterfront*, ed. Gene Desfor and Jennifer Laidley (Toronto: UT Press, 2011); and Wayne C. Reeves, "Visions for the Metropolitan Toronto Waterfront, I: Toward Comprehensive Planning, 1852–1935" (report for UT, Centre for Urban and Community Studies, 1992), 63–97.
4 "The Corporation of the City of Toronto to the Toronto Harbour Commissioners, Conveyance of Lands," 26 Dec. 1911, CTA, Fonds 2, Series 60, Item 94 (hereafter "Conveyance of Lands").
5 Blueprint, "Lakefront from Woodbine East Showing Proposed Boulevard," 21 Nov. 1912, and a larger, probably revised, version 17 Sept. 1913, are CTA, Series 724, Items 465 and 245; the CTA holds but does not permit access to these items.
6 AR of the Toronto Harbour Commissioners for 1921/22, CTA, Series 60, Item 1493, 23; BC R27, CTCMs, 1920, 1361; CTA holds a copy of what is probably this plan, 27 Nov. 1920, by Norman D. Wilson (Series 726, Item 475) but does permit viewing of it; two versions are reproduced, almost illegibly, in Reeves, "Visions for the Metropolitan Toronto Waterfront," 95.
7 For "plans," AR of the Toronto Harbour Commissioners for 1921/22, CTA, Series 60, Item 1493, 23; for "sketches," BC R27, CTCMs, 1920, 1361.
8 AR of the Toronto Harbour Commissioners for 1921/22, CTA, Series 60, Item 1493, 23.
9 This transfer is mentioned in numerous documents, including "Conveyance of Lands," 1.
10 Details about the leases and lessees are in CTA, Fonds 200, Series 769, Files 28–32.

11 "Conveyance of Lands"; "Plan of Part of Eastern Sandbar – Toronto," 1911, CTA, Series 726, Item 252; more details are in Items 253–6.
12 Multiple sources.
13 Water lots are drawn on "Plan Showing Lakefront from Woodbine Av. to East City Limit," 19 Aug. 1920, CTA, Series 726, Item 275.
14 "Scarborough Beach Park Water Lots, Etc., Purchase of," BC R15, CTCMs, 1925, 919–20.
15 CT Bylaw #8601 (20 Dec. 1920); CT Bylaw #8964 (19 Dec. 1921); also R20 of Cttee on Parks and Exhibitions, CTCMs, 1920, 1340.
16 "Scarborough Beach Park Water Lots, Etc., Purchase of," BC R15, 30 June 1925, CTCMs, 1925, 919–20.
17 Dozens of these cases are reported in CTCMs for 1928, 1929, and 1930; the arbitrator's figure was always well below what the property owners claimed.
18 Annual reports of the Toronto Harbour Commissioners, various years, CTA, Series 60, Item 1493; for Woodbine Beach clearance, 1928, 6.
19 CTCMs, 1929, index entries for Toronto Harbour Commissioners dredging.
20 "Eastern Beaches Water Front Development," BC R7, CTCMs, 1929, 536–8.
21 "Groynes at Kew Beach October 25, 1911," photograph in City Engineer's Report, 1911 (CTA, Series 1282).
22 BC R9, CTCMs, 1929, 704. The Commissioners had built and were operating Sunnyside Beach in the west end – Dale Barbour, *Undressed Toronto: From the Swimming Hole to Sunnyside, How a City Learned to Love the Beach, 1850–1935* (Winnipeg: University of Manitoba Press, 2021), 172–212.
23 RP #M490 (6 Nov. 1925), lots numbered 22–6, 68–71, 112–15, and 156–61 inclusive; CT ARs, Hubbard Blvd. south side, 1927–9.
24 CT Bylaw #11340 (26 Sept. 1927); compensation paid to owners BC R1, CTCMs, 1929, 37–8.
25 R18 of Cttee on Parks and Exhibitions, CTCMs, 1929, 2355–6. Land acquired for the athletic field was largely unbuilt in 1923, suggesting swampy terrain – Goad's Atlas 1924.
26 CT Bylaw #12467 (27 Jan. 1930).
27 "Conditions and Soundings – Woodbine Avenue East to City Limits," 17 July 1929, CTA Series 724, Item 205. This detailed scale drawing shows every structure on the waterfront prior to expropriation; many of the expropriated buildings were photographed prior to demolition – CTA, Series 372, Sub-series 3; photograph, "Beach East of McLean Ave." (CTA, Fonds 1231, Item 1282), taken in 1917, shows substantial buildings on this stretch of the Balmy Beach waterfront.
28 The City repeatedly photographed examples of this, e.g., CTA, Series 372, Sub-series 3, Item 742.
29 Inferred from multiple sources.
30 "New East End Park is Opened with Gala Festival," *The Globe*, 25 May 1932, 9; Mary Campbell and Barbara Myrvold, *The Beach in Pictures, 1793–1932* (Toronto: TPL Board, 1988), 16–17; it was initially referred to as Kew

Beach Park, but in late May the City formally named it Eastern Beaches Waterfront Park – "Council Adopts Reports of Board and Committees," *The Globe*, 31 May 1932; deliberations recounted in R12 of Cttee of Parks and Exhibitions', CTCMs, 1931, 1113–14.

31 "Proposed Improvements – Eastern Beaches," 1 June 1931, CTA Series 724, Item 291.

32 The buildings are on lots 22–6 of RP #M490; they are depicted on "Conditions and Soundings" and "Proposed Improvements" (cited above); for their retention and leasing, BC R5, CTCM, 1931, 665.

33 Kevin McConnell, *The History of the Balmy Beach Club* (privately published, n.d.), 59; "Beach Boardwalk Extension Delayed," *The Globe*, 16 April 1932, p. 2; typescript "History of Balmy Beach Park" (dated as "193?"), CTA, Series 487, File 495.

34 R4 of Cttee on Parks and Exhibitions, CTCMs, 1931, 563; "Plan Showing Additional Lands Required for Park Purposes …," 5 Feb. 1932, CTA, Series 724, Item 219.

35 First by Hugh Garner in his 1950 novel *Cabbagetown*, 2nd ed. (Toronto: McGraw-Hill Ryerson, 1968), 202–7; more recently and more tendentiously in Karen X. Tulchinsky, *The Five Books of Moses Lapinsky* (Vancouver: Polestar, 2003), 387–401.

36 Antisemitism dominates popular culture versions, e.g., Chris Bateman, "That Time Anti-Semitism Blighted Toronto," *BlogTO*, 27 July 2013, https://www.blogto.com/city/2013/07/that_time_anti-semitism_blighted_toronto/.

37 The following narrative has been crafted from near daily accounts in *The Globe* and *Toronto Daily Star*, 2 Aug. to 14 Aug. 1933; only direct quotations are cited; the two papers, known to have different political stances, draw similar pictures; the episode is well covered, with a slightly different emphasis, in Cyril Levitt and William Shaffir, *The Riot at Christie Pits*, 2nd ed. (Toronto: New Jewish Press, 2018), 53–70.

38 Cited in several newspaper accounts.

39 "Toronto "Swastikas" Arouse Jews," *Evening Telegram*, 1 Aug. 1933, p. 1, includes a photograph that now circulates online.

40 "Police Halt Possible Swastika Clash," *The Globe*, 2 Aug. 1933, p. 2.

41 "Swastika Emblems Vanish from Beach as Jews Parade There," *Toronto Daily Star*, 2 Aug. 1933, p. 11.

42 "Police Halt Possible Swastika Clash," *The Globe*, 2 Aug. 1933, p. 2.

43 "Swastika Group Will Hold Meeting with Jewish League," *The Globe*, 4 Aug. 1933, p. 9.

44 "Police Patrol Store Used by Beach Boys," *Toronto Daily Star*, 3 Aug. 1933, p. 23.

45 "Beaches in Turmoil as Swastikas Worn," *Toronto Daily Star*, 8 Aug. 1933, p. 2; *Globe* coverage is equally detailed – "Swastika Badge Urged Removed by Police Officer," *The Globe*, 7 Aug. 1933, p. 1.

46 "Police Keep Order, Both Groups Are Told by Mayor," *The Globe*, 10 Aug. 1933, pp. 9–10.

47 "Declares Swastika Emblem Like Crouching Wild Beast," *Toronto Daily Star*, 10 Aug. 1933, p. 18.
48 In 1931 7.2% of Toronto's population identified as ethnic Jewish; the next largest non-British group was Italian, 2.1% – James Lemon, *Toronto since 1918: An Illustrated History* (Toronto: Lorimer, 1985), table 7, 196.
49 This generational difference, not uncommon in diasporic communities, is noted in Stephen Speisman, "Antisemitism in Ontario: The Twentieth Century," *Antisemitism in Canada: History and Interpretations*, ed. Alan T. Davies, 114–16 (Waterloo, ON: Wilfrid Laurier University Press, 1992).
50 Kaufman is identified in several accounts as the "self-described King of Hoboes," with no explanation or source; a search of online digitized newspapers confirmed that Kaufman was for real and had indeed served for a time as the King of Hoboes, an established honorific in hobo culture; a report of an encounter in Patterson, New Jersey, is especially revealing: "Tramp Prince Breezes In, Takes Watch, Breezes Out," *Jewish Daily Bulletin*, 22 Feb. 1934, accessed at https://www.jta.org/1934/02/22/archive/tramp-prince-breezes-in-takes-watch-breezes-out.
51 "Beaches in Turmoil as Swastikas Worn," *Toronto Daily Star*, 8 Aug. 1933, p. 2.
52 "Noisy Meeting at Beach Form a New Association," *Toronto Daily Star*, 18 Aug. 1933, p. 11.
53 Morris Simkin, proprietor of a downtown printing press manufacturer, lived at 96 Kippendavie, and he remained there until the mid-1940s – TCDs.
54 Levitt and Shaffir, *Riot at Christie Pits*, makes this point in several contexts.
55 "Hitler's Aide Denies Meddling Here," *Toronto Daily Star*, 11 Aug. 1933, p. 1.
56 Levitt and Shaffir come to a similar conclusion in *Riot at Christie Pits*, 109–10.
57 We will never know the size of the "movement"; estimates range from a few dozen to a few thousand depending on the purpose of the estimate; after the main melee Ganter stated a membership of thirty-one but a "prospective membership" of thousands, and although the latter number was just his fantasy (and many other people's fears), his statement may be as close to the truth as one can get – "Swastika Movement Reported Spreading," *Toronto Daily Star*, 9 Aug. 1933, 17.
58 Benson Orenstein's memoir on the Beach Hebrew Institute website – though facts and dates seem a little off – clearly reveals both the presence and absence of local antisemitism – https://www.beachhebrewinstitute.ca/memoirs

7. The Neighbourhood Endures

1 "Population and Housing Characteristics by Census Tracts – Toronto," table 2, Census of Canada 1951; for the purposes of this research, Tracts 131, 132, 133, and 135 are considered the Beaches, although not all of 131 is in the neighbourhood as defined here. For comparison, the neighbourhood in 2016 (slightly larger than defined here) had 21,567

residents, 9,425 households, and 2.27 persons per household; in 2016, 34.7% of its households were single-person, in 1951, 5.3%.

2 Apparent in many photographs from the 1930s in CTA, Series 372, Sub-series 1 (Architect's) and 3 (Assessment).

3 Full neighbourhood: 7,009 dwellings of which 2,480 were apartments/flats; below Queen St (Tract 135): 2,306 dwellings of which 1,495 were apartments/flats. "Population and Housing Characteristics by Census Tracts – Toronto," table 2, Census of Canada 1951.

4 Harold Kalman, *A History of Canadian Architecture*, vol. 2 (Toronto: Oxford University Press, 1994), 619–24.

5 "Price Brothers Buyer Is Harry Stevens," *The Globe*, 2 July 1928, p. 12.

6 1941 population taken from the 1951 census.

7 This includes Baptists, Anglican, Presbyterian, and United Church; other Protestant sects had very small numbers.

8 Including the full Tract 131 probably exaggerates the Roman Catholic numbers.

9 Appendix, table 2, drawing from TCDs. Robert Fulford, *Accidental City: The Transformation of Toronto* (Toronto: Macfarlane Walter & Ross, 1995), 91, describes it as "lower-middle class."

10 Lorraine O'Donnell Williams, *Memories of the Beach: Reflections on a Toronto Childhood* (Toronto: Dundurn Press, 2010) portrays this well.

11 Appendix, table 2, Pine Crescent (1941).

12 An observation that goes against the grain of much American scholarship, summarized in Emily Talen, *Neighbourhood* (New York: Oxford University Press, 2019), 219–25.

13 Appendix, table 4.

14 Of 7,009 dwellings, 3,280 had a passenger car. "Population and Housing Characteristics by Census Tracts – Toronto," table 2, Census of Canada 1951.

15 Williams, *Memories of the Beach*, 33; M. Jane Fairburn, *Along the Shore: Rediscovering Toronto's Waterfront Heritage* (Toronto: ECW Press, 2013), 174–5; Robert Fulford, "Beach Boy," in *The Toronto Book*, ed. William Kilbourne, 89–98 (Toronto: Macmillan, 1976).

16 As noted in the introduction, this interpretation is informed by Suzanne Keller, *The Urban Neighborhood: A Sociological Perspective*, Studies in Sociology (New York: Random House, 1968), 77–123.

17 This excludes two major Roman Catholic churches built just outside the neighbourhood.

18 Williams, *Memories of the Beach*, is full of these; her experiences with the drama league (chapter 29) and square dance group (chapter 30), 202–19, are especially striking.

19 Kevin McConnell, *The History of the Balmy Beach Club* (self-published, 2012), 49–63; Fulford, *Accidental City*, 97.

20 Also observed in Sam Bass Warner, *Streetcar Suburbs: The Process of Growth in Boston (1870–1900)* (Cambridge, MA: Harvard University Press, 1962), 158–9.

21 Elena Ferrante, *Those Who Leave and Those Who Stay* (New York: Europa Editions, 2014), 24.
22 Elena Ferrante, *The Story of a Lost Child* (New York: Europa Editions, 2015), 460.
23 Keith Black, *Boom: A Child of the Beach in Toronto Remembers the 50's* (self-published, 2020), 191–2.
24 "Population and Housing Characteristics by Census Tracts – Toronto," table 1, Census of Canada 1951, 1961, and 1971, Tracts 131, 132, 133, and 135 in the 1951 and 1961 census, renumbered as Tracts 24, 23, 22, and 21 in the 1971 census.
25 James Lemon, *Toronto since 1918: An Illustrated History* (Toronto: Lorimer, 1985), table 8, 196.
26 Jim Sanderson, *Life in Balmy Beach: Growing Up in Toronto in the 1950s and '60s* (self-published [Xlibris], 2018), 123.
27 Calculated by author from "Population and Housing Characteristics by Census Tracts – Toronto," table 1, Census of Canada 1951, 1961, and 1971; total Italian population for the four census tracts in 1971 was 700, of which 465 resided in Tract 24 (formerly 131); Jewish "Religion," cited here, is slightly higher than Jewish "Origin" (0.4%) in the census, suggesting that Canadian-born Jews did not all identify as being of Jewish "origin."
28 Fulford, "Beach Boy," 90; Keith Black notes the same in his memoir – Black, *Boom*, 172, as does Jim Sanderson in his, *Life in Balmy Beach.*
29 Glenn Cochrane and Jean Cochrane, *The Beach: An Illustrated History from the Lake to Kingston Road* (Toronto: ECW Press, 2009), 37, recounts one such incident.
30 Richard Harris states that "ethnic covenants shaped the patterns of settlement in many Canadian urban areas." If this generalization is true – he cites no specific evidence – then the Beaches was unusually unrestrictive. Richard Harris, *Creeping Conformity: How Canada Became Suburban, 1900–1960* (Toronto: UT Press), 89.
31 Appendix, table 2, Waverley Road (1951) and Willow Avenue (1961).
32 Calculated by author from "Population and Housing Characteristics by Census Tracts – Toronto," table 2, Census of Canada 1961 and 1971.
33 Alvin Finkel highlights this, on a national scale, in *Our Lives: Canada after 1945*, 2nd ed. (Toronto: Lorimer, 2012), especially 9–10.
34 Ownership was not reported in the earlier TCDs and was therefore not comprehensively compiled, but it was shown and proved to be useful for these later years.
35 See Appendix, table 2.
36 "All the Toronto beach areas with the exception of the Island beaches were closed in the summer of 1959," Ontario, OWRC, "Water Quality and Water Pollution in Metropolitan Toronto along Lake Ontario 1964–65," 8.
37 McConnell, *The History of the Balmy Beach Club*, 128; a photograph of the clubhouse before it burned is "Balmy Beach Club, Balmy Beach Park," 1953, TPL, Digital Archive, PICTURES-R-5451.

38 Ontario Land Registry Office, Historical Books, Toronto Section 'S', Vol. 1, Parcel 1, Folios 6–7; "Proposed Subdivision of … Plan 315," 4 July 1944, CTA, Fonds 2032, Series 727, Item 52; CTA, aerial photographs of Toronto, 1947, 50, 53, and 56; TCDs, 1942, 45, 47, and 50.

39 "Neighbourhood Classifications," *Third Annual Report of the City Planning Board*, Toronto, 31 Dec. 1944, covered in Richard White, *Planning Toronto: The Planners, The Plans, Their Legacies, 1940–80* (Vancouver: UBC Press, 2016), 35–42.

40 The neighbourhood population rose slightly from 1941 (26,393) to 1951 (26,704) then declined slightly to 1961 (26,165). "Population and Housing Characteristics by Census Tracts – Toronto," table 1, Census of Canada 1951 (which includes 1941 figures) and 1961. For context, White, "The Absence of Decline," in *Planning Toronto*, 147–50.

41 Sanderson, *Life in Balmy Beach*, portrays this well.

42 TCD, 1961, Neville Park Boulevard.

43 TCDs. Directories usually noted ownership in these later years, and this statement is based on findings for Waverley Road (1951), Balsam Avenue (1951), Scarborough Beach Boulevard (1961), and Willow Avenue (1961).

44 Appendix, table 2; ownership also from TCD, 1961, Willow Avenue.

45 Richard Harris, *Building a Market: The Rise of the Home Improvement Industry, 1914–1960* (Chicago: University of Chicago Press, 2012), 202–5. As an entire generation of owners has now learned, rehabilitating an old house requires major investment.

46 One informal interviewee, who grew up on Beech Avenue in the 1950s, recalled her father opting to sell their aging house because its roof leaked.

47 David Ley, "'Follow the Hippies': The Cultural Politics of Gentrification," in *The New Middle Class and the Remaking of the Central City*, 176–221 (Oxford: Oxford University Press, 1996); Jim Sanderson offers his first experience with the counterculture in "Beatniks!," *Life in Balmy Beach*, 44–53.

48 Fulford, *Accidental City*, 92.

49 Changes are well summarized in Mary Campbell and Barbara Myrvold, *Historical Walking Tour of Kew Beach* (Toronto: TPL Board, 1995), 10; other Toronto neighbourhoods changed in this way too – changes were underway in urban society generally.

50 The 1971 population (25,320) shows a small but not insignificant decline (1961: 26,165) – "Population and Housing Characteristics by Census Tracts – Toronto," table 1, Census of Canada, 1971 and 1961; by 1996, population, for a larger area, had fallen to 19,035 – CT Neighbourhood Profiles, accessed at Neighbourhood Profiles – City of Toronto.

51 Campbell and Myrvold, *Historical Walking Tour*, 10, 17.

52 Suzanne Keller, *The Urban Neighbourhood: A Sociological Perspective*, Studies in Sociology (New York: Random House, 1968), 106, 119.

53 In the 1970s, as a form of assisted housing, the City Housing Department bought individual houses in the neighbourhood and rented them to low-income tenants; some small seniors' homes were also built.

54 For the former (south side of Queen Street between Lee and Leuty Avenues), Campbell and Myrvold, *Historical Walking Tour*, 34; for the latter (west side of Beech Avenue, south of Queen, on which later was built El Pueblo apartments), "Report on Proposed Amendment … Beech Avenue," 5 Feb. 1963, City of Toronto Planning Board Minutes, CTA, Series 719, Files 40 and 41.

55 Leaving "physical character" undefined – "Policies," No. 7, "City of Toronto Official Plan," updated and consolidated February 2019, p. 2-19; for the origins of this in the 1969 plan, White, *Planning Toronto*, 214–17.

56 "Ontario Heritage Act," *Revised Statutes of Ontario*, 1980, Chapter 337, Part V, 988–90.

57 ERA Architects, "Kingswood Road South Heritage Conservation District," 5 June 2009.

58 In 2001, self-attributed English, Scottish, Irish, and *Canadian* ethnicity, added altogether, was approximately 77% of Beaches population (Toronto approximately 50%); the Beaches was 18.5% "immigrants" (Toronto was 49.4%) and 7.8% "visible minority" (Toronto 42.8%) – CT Neighbourhood Profile, 2001.

59 The author lives across the street from such a house.

8. Conclusion

1 Among the classics informing this analysis are D.W. Meinig, "Symbolic Landscapes: Some Idealizations of American Communities," and Peirce F. Lewis, "Axioms for Reading the Landscape: Some Guides to the American Scene," both in *The Interpretation of Ordinary Landscapes*, ed. D.W. Meinig (New York and Oxford: Oxford University Press, 1979); and especially Edward Relph, *The Modern Urban Landscape* (Baltimore: Johns Hopkins University Press, 1987). The field of landscape studies has evolved into something no longer applicable to the ideas and methods employed here, notably its preoccupation with rural landscapes and its focus on preservation; the contemporary field is well explained in Peter J. Howard, "Landscape as Culture," *An Introduction to Landscape* (Farnham, UK, and Burlington, VT: Ashgate, 2011).

2 The sources of points made earlier in the book are not restated here.

3 Jane Jacobs, "The Uses of Neighbourhood Parks," in *The Death and Life of Great American Cities* (New York: Random House, 1961), 89–111.

4 Following the essential Sam Bass Warner, *Streetcar Suburbs: The Process of Growth in Boston (1870–1900)* (Cambridge, MA: Harvard University Press, 1962), 75.

5 The house is "listed" by the City and noted by the Architectural Conservatory of Ontario; neither mentions significant alterations since 1947.

6 Adam Rome, *The Bulldozer in the Countryside: Suburban Sprawl and the Rise of American Environmentalism* (Cambridge: Cambridge University Press, 2001); Francesca Russello Ammon, *Bulldozer: Demolition and Clearance of the Postwar Landscape* (New Haven, CT: Yale University Press, 2016).

7 Streams are shown crossing Queen Street at Neville Park Boulevard (RP #389E), Willow Avenue (RP #406), Balsam Road/Maclean Avenue (RP #406), on the Kew Gardens property (RP #90), and at Kenilworth Avenue (RP #M28); see also figure 1, above.
8 Marjorie Howard, "The History of the Beaches District," n.d. (c. 1938), handwritten essay, TPL, Beaches Branch, Scrapbook, Local History Collection.
9 Glen Cochrane and Jean Cochrane, *The Beach: An Illustrated History from the Lake to Kingston Road* (Toronto: ECW Press, 2009), 109–10; the precise date of draining could not be determined.
10 RP #M218 (28 July 1903), Mary I. Gray property owner; Goad's Atlas 1910, 1913, and 1924; TCDs, 1905, 1908, and 1910.
11 Photographs, CTA, Series 376, Sub-series 5, Items 58 and 59; Series 372, Sub-series 58, Items 912–20; Goad's Atlas 1924.
12 Cathy Commins, "A History of Balmy Beach," *Ward 9 News*, April 1980 (2nd instalment), TPL, Beaches Branch, Local History Collection.
13 Ted Reeve, "More Beach Reminiscences," in TPL, Beaches Branch, Scrapbooks, Local History Collection, presents a vivid picture of these now vanished wetlands.
14 Tom Whillans, "Waterfront Ecosystems: Restoring is Remembering," in *Special Places: The Changing Ecosystems of the Toronto Region*, ed. Betty I. Roots, et al. (Vancouver: UBC Press 1999), 245–8 (p. 247 for statistic).
15 A central theme of M. Jane Fairburn, *Along the Shore: Rediscovering Toronto's Waterfront Heritage* (Toronto: ECW Press, 2013).
16 Photograph, "Looking south from Kew Beach firehall," 1906, CTA, Series 376, File 5, Item 34.
17 James E. Eckenwalder, "Vascular Plants," in Roots, *Special Places*, 107–10.
18 "Beaches Library Scrapbooks: Churches," in TPL, Beaches Branch, Local History Collection, contains a wealth of ephemera and anecdotal histories pertaining to the neighbourhood churches.
19 "History," Beach Hebrew Institute website: www.beachhebrewinstitute.ca/.
20 Brought to mind by Roberto Perin, "Fulsome Fellowship, 1880–1920," in *The Many Rooms of This House: Diversity in Toronto's Places of Worship since 1840* (Toronto: UT Press, 2017), 84–121.
21 "Beach Hebrew Institute: Early History" (drawing from oral histories), accessed at http://ontariojewisharchives.org/exhibits/synagogues/synogogues/Beach/history.html.
22 Hugh Garner's fictional antisemite in *Cabbagetown*, 2nd ed. (Toronto: McGraw-Hill Ryerson, 1968), 207, complains about this tolerance, calling the residents "good solid Anglo Saxon Orangemen, pretty insular and stupid actually."
23 Lorraine O'Donnell Williams, author of *Memories of the Beach*, grew up Roman Catholic in the 1940s; though her faith set her apart she recounts no overt antipathy, and her best friend was United Church.
24 Ontario Land Registry Office, Historical Books, Toronto Section "S", Parcel 1, Folio 4; St. John Catholic School opened on Kingston Road, just north of the neighbourhood, in 1910.

25 Household size for 1900: "The Shift to Smaller Households over the Past Century," at Statistics Canada website, https://www150.statcan.gc.ca/n1/pub/11-630-x/11-630-x2015008-eng.htm; for 2016, the neighbourhood profile at www.toronto.ca/ext/sdfa/Neighbourhood%20Profiles/pdf/2016/pdf1/cpa63.pdf.
26 From his *The Theory of the Leisure Class: An Economic Study of Institutions*, published in 1899.
27 One can infer this from the occupations of occupants in TCDs.
28 "The Beaches Become a Populous Suburb," *Toronto Daily Star*, 21 April 1906, p. 12.
29 "Swastika Spokesman of German Descent," *Toronto Daily Star*, 5 Aug. 1933, p. 3.
30 Various directories and assessment rolls.
31 Commins, "A History of Balmy Beach."
32 E.g., "Pine Terrace," Photograph, 12 Oct. 1939, CTA, Series 372, Sub-series 33, Item 625.

Appendix

1 Accessed at www.torontopubliclibrary.ca/history-genealogy/lh-digital-city-directories.jsp.

Index